Dog Parks Unleashed

A Directory of Local Dog Parks

United States

Edition

Deanna L. Taber

Dog Parks Unleashed, A Directory Of Local Dog Parks.
United States Edition

Copyright © by Deanna L. Taber

Cover design by Deanna L. Taber

Printed in the United States of America

All rights reserved. No part of this publication may be reproduced or transmitted in any form or by any means, electronic or mechanical, including photocopy, recording, or any information storage and retrieval system, without permission in writing from the copyright owner and the publisher of this book.

February 2010

ISBN- 1451517157

EAN-13- 9781451517156

This is dedicated to every dog owner. May you and your four legged friend have a great day at the park.

Acknowledgment

I would like to thank everyone who gave me love and or support. Thank you for allowing me to follow my dream.

Table Of Contents

Western States

Alaska	2
Arizona	3-18
California	19-68
Colorado	69-80
Hawaii	81-82
Idaho	83-84
Montana	85-86
Nevada	87-92
New Mexico	93-96
Oregon	97-103
Utah	104-107
Washington	108-118
Wyoming	119

Central States

Arkansas	120-121
Illinois	122-138
Iowa	139-142
Kansas	143-146
Louisiana	147-149
Minnesota	150-161
Mississippi	162
Missouri	163-170
Nebraska	171-174
North Dakota	175-176
Oklahoma	177-179

South Dakota..180
Texas..181-196
Wisconsin..197-207

Eastern States

Alabama..208-209
Connecticut...210-214
Delaware...215
Florida..216-245
Georgia...246-254
Indiana..255-264
Kentucky...265-269
Maine..270-271
Maryland...272-280
Massachusetts..281-285
Michigan...286-297
New Hampshire..298-299
New Jersey..300-307
New York..308-324
North Carolina...325-335
Ohio...336-351
Pennsylvania..352-369
Rhode Island..370-371
South Carolina...372-376
Tennessee..377-381
Vermont..382-383
Virginia...384-394
Washington D.C..395
West Virginia...396-397

ALASKA

F

FAIRBANKS

Fairbanks Dog Park

Address: Corner of Wilber and Davis

ARIZONA

A
AVONDALE
Friendship Dog Park
Address: 12325 West McDowell Road
Phone: 623-478-3050
Hours: Open daily 5:00 am to 11:00 pm.

C
CHANDLER
Shawnee Bark Park
Address: 1400 West Mesquite Street North
Phone: 480-782-2727 or 480-782-2640
Hours: Open 7 days a week from 6:00 am to 10:30 pm. Closed Tuesdays from 6:00 am to 2:30 pm for cleaning.

Snedigar Sportsplex
Address: 4500 South Basha Road
Phone: 480-782-2727 or 480-782-2640
Hours: Open 7 days a week from 6:00 am to 10:30 pm. Closed Wednesdays from 6:00 am to 2:30 pm for cleaning.

West Chandler Bark Park
Address: 250 South Kyrene Road
Phone: 480-782-2727 or 480-782-2640
Hours: Open 7 days a week from 6:00 am to 10:30 pm. Closed Monday and Wednesday from 6:00 am to 2:30 pm for cleaning.

Paseo Vista Recreation Area (Coming Soon)
Address: McQueen and Ocotillo Roads.

C

COTTONWOOD

Cottonwood Dog Park

Address: Riverfront Park Drive, North 10th Street

Hours: Open sunrise to sunset. Closed Tuesdays until 9:00 am.

F

FLAGSTAFF

Bushmaster Park

Address: 3150 North Alta Vista

Phone: 928-773-0645

Flagstaff Dog Park at Thorpe Park

Address: 191 Thorpe Road

Phone: 928-213-2300

FLORENCE

Florence Dog Park
Address: 200 East Eighth Street

FOUNTAIN HILLS

Desert Vista Neighborhood Dog Park
Address: Saguaro Boulevard and Desert Vista Drive
Hours: Open 6:00 am to 9:00 pm daily.

G

GILBERT

Cosmo Dog Park
Address: 2502 East Ray Road
Hours: Open 5:30 am to 10:00 pm daily.

Crossroads Dog Park
Address: 2155 East Knox Road
Hours: Open 5:30 am to 10:00 pm daily.

GLENDALE

Sahuaro Ranch Park

Address: 63rd Avenue and Mountain View Road

Phone: 623-930-2820

Hours: Open 6:00 am to 10:00 pm daily.

Foothills Park

Address: 57th Avenue and Union Hills Drive

Phone: 623-930-2820

Northern Horizon Dog Park

Address: 63rd and Northern Avenue

GOODYEAR

Goodyear Dog Park

Address: 15600 West Roeser

K

KINGMAN

Lewis Kingman Dog Park

Address: 2201 East Andy Devine Avenue

L

Lake Havasu

Lion's Dog Park

Address: 1340 McCulloch Boulevard

Hours: Open 24 hours a day.

M

MARANA

San Lucas Community Dog Park

Address: 14040 North Adonis Road

Silverbell-Cortaro Dog Park

Address: 7548 North Silverbell Road

MESA

Quail Run Park

Address: 4155 East Virginia Street

Hours: Closed all day Thursdays.

P

PAYSON

Rumsey Dog Park

Address: McLane Road next to the library.

PHOENIX

Echo Mountain Off Leash Area

Address: 17447 North 20th Street

Phone: 602-262-6696

Hours: Closed on irrigation days.

RJ Dog Park at Pecos Park
Address: 48th Street and Pecos Parkway
Phone: 602-534-5252
Hours: Open 6:00 am to 11:00 pm daily. Closed on irrigation days.

Steele Indian School Dog Park
Address: East Indian School Road and 7th Street
Hours: Open 6:00 am to 11:00 pm daily. Closed on irrigation days.

Pet Smart Dog Park
Address: 21st Avenue between Bethany Home Road and Glendale Road.
Phone: 602-262-6971
Hours: Open 6:30 am to 10:00 pm daily.

Rose Mofford Sports Complex Dog Park
Address: 9833 North 25th Avenue
Phone: 602-261-8011
Hours: Open 6:30 am to 10:00 pm. Closed on irrigation days or heavy rain.

PRESCOTT

Jim McCasland Willow Creek Dog Park
Address: 3181 Willow Creek Road
Phone: 928-771-5899
Hours: Open 7:00 am to 10:00 pm in winter. Open 5:00 am to 10:00 pm in summer.

SAHUARITA

Quail Creek Dog Park
Address: 1905 South Old Nogales Highway
Hours: Open from dawn to dusk.

Anamax Dog Park
Address: 15701 South Camino de las Quintas
Hours: Closed from 10:30 am to 12:30 pm Tuesdays and Fridays for regular maintenance.

SCOTTSDALE
Horizon Park
Address: 15444 North 100th Street
Phone: 480-312-2650
Hours: Open dawn to 10:30 pm. Closed Thursdays from 9:30 am to 12:30 pm.

Scottsdale Off Leash Activity Center
Address: North Hayden Road and East McDonald Drive
Hours: Open 6:00 am to 9:00 pm daily.

Chaparral Park
Address: 541 North Hayden Road
Phone: 480-312-2353
Hours: November 1 through April 30, 6:00 am to 10:00 pm daily. May 1 through October 31, 5:30 am to 10:00 pm daily.

Vista del Camino Park
Address: 7700 East Roosevelt Street
Hours: Open 5:30 am to 10:00 pm daily.

SEDONA
Sedona Dog Park
Address: NW Corner of Carruth and Soldiers Pass Roads.
Phone: 928-301-0226

SHOWLOW

The Deuce of Dogs Bark Park

Address: Deuce of Clubs Road and State Route 260

SURPRISE

Surprise Dog Park

Address: 15930 North Bullard Avenue

Hours: Open 6:00 am to 10:00 pm daily.

T

TEMPE

Mitchell Park

Address: 900 South Mitchell Drive

Phone: 480-350-5200

Hours: Open 6:00 am to midnight. Closed Thursdays.

Creamery Park

Address: 8th Street and Una Avenue

Hours: Open 6:00 am to 10:00 pm daily.

Jaycee Park
Address: 5th Street and Hardy Drive
Hours: Open 6:00 am to 10:00 pm daily.

Papago Dog Park
Address: Curry Road and College Avenue
Hours: Open 6:00 am to 10:00 pm daily.

Tempe Sports Complex Dog Park
Address: Warner Road and Hardy Drive
Hours: Open 6:00 am to 10:00 pm daily.

T
TUSCON
Brandi Fenton Dog Park
Address:3482 East River Road
Phone: 520-232-1201
Hours: Open 7:00 am to 10:00 pm daily.

Jacobs Dog Park
Address: 330 North Fairview Avenue
Phone: 520-791-4873

Northwest Community Dog Park
Address: 7601 North Mona Lisa Road
Phone: 520-877-6000

Palo Verde Dog Park
Address: 300 South Mann Avenue
Phone: 520-877-6000

Udall Dog Park
Address: 7290 East Tanque Verde
Phone: 520-791-5930
Hours: Open 6:00 am to 10 pm daily.

Christopher Columbus Park
Address: 4600 North Silverbell
Phone: 520-791-4873
Hours: Open sunrise to sunset.

Humane Society Dog Park and Training Field
Address: 3465 East Kleindale
Hours: Open 5:00 am to 9:00 am and 5:00 pm to 9:00 pm daily.

McDonald Park
Address: 4100 North Harrison Road
Phone: 520-877-6211
Hours: Open sunrise to sunset.

Gene C. Reid Park
Address: Country Club and 22nd Street
Phone: 520-791-4873 ext 141
Hours: Open 7:00 am to 9:00 pm daily.

North Sixth Avenue Park
Address: 2075 North 6th Avenue
Phone: 520-791-4873
Hours: Open sunrise to sunset daily.

Y

YUMA

Yuma Dog Park

Address: 1705 East Palo Verde Street

Hours: Open Wednesday through Monday, dawn to 9:00 pm. Closed Tuesdays.

CALIFORNIA

A

ALAMEDA

Main Street Linear Dog Park
Address: Main Street and Atlantic Avenue

Washington Small Dog Park
Address: 740 Central Avenue

AMERICAN CANYON

American Canyon Dog Park
Address: Broadway Street

APTOS

Aptos Dog Park
Address: 2255 Huntington Avenue
Hours: Open sunrise to sunset daily.

ARCADIA

Arcadia Dog Park

Address: Second Avenue and Colorado Boulevard

Hours: Open 7:00 am to dusk daily.

ARROYO GRANDE

Elm Street Dog Park

Address: 1221 Ash Street

ATASCADERO

Heilmann Regional Dog Park

Address: 10000 El Bordo Avenue

AUBURN

Ashley Memorial Dog Park

Address: Auburn Ravine Road

ERSFIELD

ennial Dog Park
ess: Montclair Street

og Park
s: Kroll and Maltavo

ty Dog Park
: University Avenue

og Park
Wilson Road and Hughes Lane

IT

k Community Dog Park
0 West Oak Valley Parkway
845-9555

BELMONT

Cipriani Dog Park

Address: 2525 Buena Vista and Monserat Avenue

Hours: Open sunrise to 8:30 pm daily.

BENICIA

The Phenix Community Dog Park

Address: Rose Drive

BERKELEY

Ohlone Dog Park

Address: Grant Street and Hearst Avenue

Hours: Open 6:00 am to 10 pm (Mon-Fri) and 9:00 am to 10:00 pm (Sat-Sun and Holidays).

BRISBANE

Brisbane Dog Park

Address: 50 Park Place

BUENA PARK

Bellis Dog Park

Address: 7171 8th Street

Hours: Open 8:00 am to dusk. Closed Wednesdays.

BURLINGAME

Bayside Dog Exercise Park

Address: 1125 Airport Boulevard

Hours: Open 6:00 am to 9:00 pm. Closed Wednesday 7:00 am to 9:00 am.

C

CALABASAS

Calabasas Bark Park

Address: 4232 Las Virgenes Road

Hours: Open 5:00 am to 9:00 pm daily.

CAMBRIA

Cambria Dog Park

Address: Main Street and Santa Rosa Creek Road

CAMPBELL

Los Gatos Creek Dog Park

Address: 1250 Dell Avenue

Phone: 408-355-2200

Hours: Open 8:00 am to sunset. Closed Tuesday until 11:00 am.

CARLSBAD

Ann D. L' Heureux Memorial Dog Park

Address: Carlsbad Village Drive

Phone: 760-434-2825

CARMICHAEL

Canine Corral Dog Park

Address: 5750 Grant Avenue

Hours: Open 5:00 am to 11:00 pm daily.

CASTRO VALLEY

Earl Warren Dog Park

Address: 4660 Crow Canyon Road

Phone: 510-881-6700

Hours: Open sunrise to sunset.

CHULA VISTA

Montevalle Dog Park

Address: 840 Duncan Ranch Road

Phone: 619-691-5269

Otay Ranch Town Center Dog Park

Address: Town Center Drive and Olympic Parkway

Phone: 619-656-9100

Hours: Open 6:00 am to 11:00 pm daily.

Veterans Dog Park

Address: 785 East Palomar

Phone: 619-691-5260

CITRUS HEIGHTS
C-Bar-C Dog Park
Address: Oak Avenue
Hours: Open daily from 8:00 am to 6:00 pm.

CLAYTON
Clayton Dog Park
Address: Marsh Creek Road
Hours: Open sunrise to sunset daily.

COLMA
Colma Dog Park
Address: End of D Street
Phone: 650-985-5678

CONCORD
The Paw Patch Dog Park
Address: Ayers Road and Turtle Creek Road
Phone: 925-671-3329
Hours: Open sunrise to sunset. Closed Wednesdays.

CORONA

Corona Dog Park
Address: 1886 Butterfield Drive

Dairyland Dog Park
Address: 14520 San Remo

Parkview Meadows Dog Park
Address: 65th and Hellman

COSTA MESA

Costa Mesa Bark Park
Address: 890 Arlington Drive
Hours: Open dawn to 9:00 pm Wednesday through Monday. Closed Tuesdays for maintenance.

CRESTLINE

Lake Gregory Dog Park
Address: 24171 Lake Drive
Phone: 909-338-4590

CULVER CITY

The Boneyard

Address: Corner of Duquesne and Jefferson

Hours: Open sunrise to sunset.

D
DANVILLE

Canine Corral Dog Park

Address: 1029 La Gonda Way

DAVIS

Community Park Dog Park

Address: 1405 F Street

Toad Hollow Dog Park

Address: 1919 Second Street

DUBLIN

Dougherty Hills Dog Park

Address: Amador Valley Boulevard and Stagecoach Road

E

EASTVALE

Harada Heritage Dog Park
Address: 13100 65th Street

EL CAJON

Wells Dog Park
Address: 1153 East Madison Avenue
Hours: Open daily 7:00 am to 9:00 pm daily.

ELK GROVE

Elk Grove Dog Park
Address: 9950 Elk Grove-Florin Road
Hours: Open sunrise to sunset.

Morse Dog Park
Address: 5540 Bellaterra Drive

EL SEGUNDO

El Segundo Dog Park

Address: East Imperial Avenue

ENCINITAS

Cricket's Corner Dog Park

Address: 389 Requeza Street

Hours: Open Tuesday and Thursday 2:00 pm to 5:00 pm. Open Friday and Saturday 11:00 am to 5:00 pm.

ENCINO

Sepulveda Basin Dog Park

Address: 17550 Victory Boulevard

Phone: 818-756-7667

Hours: Open sunrise to sunset daily. Closed Fridays sunrise to 11:00 am.

F

FAIR OAKS

Phoenix Dog Park

Address 9050 Sunset Avenue

Phone: 916-966-1036

FOLSOM

FIDO Field-Folsom Dog Park

Address: 1780 Creekside Drive

Hours: Open Thursday through Monday. Closed Tuesday and Wednesday.

FOSTER CITY

Foster City Dog Park

Address: 600 Foster City Boulevard

Hours: Open 6:00 am to 10:00 pm daily.

FREMONT

Central Park Dog Park

Address: 1110 Stevenson Boulevard

Hours: Open sunrise to 10:00 pm daily.

FRESNO

El Capitan Basin AH1 Dog Park

Address: 4257 West Alamos

Hours: Open 7:00 am to 10:00 pm (May- Nov). Closed December through April.

Roeding Park Dog Park

Address: 890 West Belmont

Hours: Open 6:00 am to 10:00 pm daily.

Woodward Park Dog Park

Address: 7775 Friant Road

Hours: Open 6:00 am to 10:00 pm daily.

FULLERTON

Fullerton Pooch Park

Address: 201 South Basque Avenue

Hours: Open 7:00 am to 8:00 pm daily. Closed Wednesday.

G

GALT

Monterey Dog Park-Galt Bark Park

Address: 1170 Monterey Bay Court

GARDEN GROVE

Garden Grove Dog Park

Address: 9301 Westminster Boulevard

Hours: Open sunrise to sunset.

GILROY

Las Animas Dog Park

Address: 400 Mantelli Drive

H

HUNTINGTON BEACH

Huntington Beach Dog Beach

Address: Pacific Coast Highway between 21st Street and Seapoint Street

Hours: Open 5:00 am to 8:00 pm daily.

Huntington Central Park Dog Park

Address: Edwards Street

Phone: 714-536-5672

Hours: Open 9:00 am to 7:00 pm, Monday through Friday and 10:00 am to 7:00 pm weekends.

HALF MOON BAY

Coast Side Dog Park

Address: Wavecrest Road

Hours: Open sunrise to sunset daily.

I

IRVINE

Central Bark Dog Park

Address: 6405 Oak Canyon

Phone: 949-724-6833

Hours: Open 6:30 am to 10:00 pm. Closed Wednesdays for maintenance.

L

LADERA RANCH

Wagsdale Dog Park

Address: O'Neill Drive at Cecil Pasture Road

Hours: Open dawn until 10:00 pm. Closed Tuesdays from 10:00 am until 1:00 pm.

LAGUNA

Laguna Community Dog Park

Address: 9014 Bruceville Road

Hours: Open sunrise to sunset.

LAGUNA BEACH

Laguna Beach Dog Park

Address: Laguna Canyon Road

Hours: Open Thursday through Tuesday from dawn to dusk. Closed Wednesday for maintenance.

LAGUNA NIGUEL

Laguna Niguel Pooch Park

Address: Golden Lantern near Chapparosa Park

LAGUNA WOODS

Laguna Woods Dog Park

Address: Ridge Route

Hours: Open 8:00 am to 7:00 pm daily.

LA MESA

Harry Griffen Dog Park

Address: 9550 Milden Street

LANCASTER

Forrest E. Hull Park Off Leash Area
Address: 2850 West Avenue and L-12
Hours: Open 6:00 am to 10:00 pm daily.

LATHROP

Lathrop Dog Park
Address: 17801 Inland Passage Way
Phone: 209-941-7360

LINCOLN

Auburn Ravine Dog Park
Address: 1300 Green Ravine Drive

LIVERMORE

Marlin A. Pound Dog Park
Address: 2010 Bluebell Drive

Max Baer Dog Park
Address: 1310 Murdell Lane

May Nissen Dog Park
Address: 685 Rincon Avenue

Bruno Canziani Dog Park
Address: South Charlotte Way

Vista Meadows Park
Address: 2450 Westminster Way

LODI

Beckman Dog Park
Address: 1426 West Century Boulevard

Vinewood Dog Park
Address: 1824 West Tokay Street

LOMA LINDA

Hulda Crooks Dog Park
Address: Beaumont Avenue and Mountain View Avenue

LONG BEACH

K-9 Corner Dog Park
Address: 9th and Pacific Avenue

Lincoln Dog Park
Address: 333 West Ocean Boulevard
Hours: Open 6:00 am to dusk.

Recreation Dog Park
Address: 5201 East 7th Street
Hours: Open 6:00 am to 10:00 pm. Closed Monday 6:00 am to noon.

LOS ALAMITOS

Seal Beach Arbor Dog Park
Address: 4665 Lampson Avenue
Hours: Open sunrise to sunset.

LOS ANGELES

Barrington Dog Park
Address: 333 South Barrington Avenue
Phone: 310-476-4866
Hours: Open 5:00 am to 10:30 pm. Closed Tuesday morning until 10:00 am.

Silverlake Dog Park
Address: 1850 West Silver Lake Drive
Phone: 323-644-3946
Hours: Open 6:00 am to 10:00 pm (Mon- Thurs, Sat & Sun). Tuesday and Friday 8:30 am to 10:00 pm.

Griffith Dog Park
Address: North Zoo Drive
Phone: 323-644-6204
Hours: Open daily 5:00 am to 10:30 pm.

Runyon Canyon Dog Park
Address: 2000 North Fuller Avenue
Phone: 323-666-5046
Hours: Open sunrise to sunset.

Hermon Dog Park
Address 5566 Via Marisol
Phone: 323-255-0370
Hours: Open sunrise to sunset.

M

MENLO PARK

Nealon Dog Park
Address: 800 Middle Avenue
Hours: Open 8:00 am to 10:00 am. Closed Saturday and Sunday.

Willow Oaks Dog Park
Address: Willow Road and Coleman
Hours: Open 7:00 am to 9:00 am and 4:00 pm to dusk.

MILIPITAS

Animal Community Center Dog Park

Address: 901 Ames Avenue

Hours: Open Monday through Friday 1:00 pm to dusk. Saturday through Sunday 8:00 am to 8:00 pm.

Ed Levin Dog Park

Address: 3100 Calaveras Road

Phone: 408-262-6980

Hours: Open 8:00 am to sunset daily.

MONTEREY

El Estero Dog Park

Address: East Pearl Street and 3rd Street

Hours: Open sunrise to sunset.

MORGAN HILL

Morgan Hill Dog Park

Address: Edmundson Avenue

Hours: Open sunrise to sunset.

MORRO BAY

Del Mar Park

Address: Sequoia and Main

MOUNTAIN VIEW

Shoreline Dog Park

Address: Bill Graham Parkway at North Shoreline Boulevard

Phone: 650-903-6392

Hours: Open 6:00 am to half an hour after sunset.

N

NAPA

Alston Park Canine Commons Dog Park

Address: Dry Creek Road off of Redwood Road

Hours: Open sunrise to sunset.

NIPOMO

Nipomo Regional Dog Park

Address: Pomeroy and Teft

NORTH HOLLYWOOD

Whitnall Dog Park
Address: 5801 ½ Whitnall Highway
Phone: 818-756-8190
Hours: Open sunrise to sunset.

NOVATO

Dogbone Meadows at O'Hair Park
Address: Novato Boulevard and Sutro Avenue
Hours: Open sunrise to sunset daily.

Marin Humane Society Dog Park
Address: 171 Bel Marin Keys Boulevard
Phone: 415-883-4621
Hours: Open Tuesday, Thursday through Sunday 10:00 am to 5:30 pm. Wednesday 10:00 am to 7:00 pm.

O

OAKLAND

Gizmoland and Joaquin Miller Dog Park
Address: 3300 Joaquin Miller Road
Phone: 510-531-9597

Mosswood Dog Park
Address: Webster and 36th Street

Hardy Dog Park
Address: 491 Hardy Street

OCEANSIDE

Oceanside Humane Society Dog Park
Address: 2905 San Luis Rey Road
Hours: Open 7:00 am to 7:00 pm, Thursday through Tuesday. Closed Wednesday and for 24 hours after rain.

ORANGE

Yorba Dog Park

Address: 190 South Yorba Street

Hours: Open 7:00 am to dusk daily.

ORCUTT

Rice Ranch Community Dog Park

Address: Orcutt Community Park

Hours: Open 8:00 am to sunset daily.

P

PALM DESSERT

Civic Center Dog Park

Address: Fred Waring Drive and San Pablo Avenue

Freedom Dog Park

Address: 77-400 Country Club Drive

Joe Mann Dog Park

Address: 77-810 California Drive

University Dog Park
Address: 74802 University Park Drive

PALM SPRINGS

Palm Springs Dog Park
Address: 222 Civic Drive North
Phone: 760-322-8362

PALO ALTA

Greer Dog Park
Address: 1098 Amarillo Avenue

Hoover Dog Park
Address: 2901 Cowper Street

Mitchell Dog Park
Address: 600 East Meadow

PARADISE
Moore Road Dog Park
Address: 6705 Moore Road

PASADENA
Alice's Dog Park
Address: 3026 East Orange Grove Boulevard and Sunny Slope Avenue
Hours: Open sunrise to sunset.

PATTERSON
T.W Patterson Sports Complex Dog Park
Address: 16651 Ward Avenue

PETALUMA
Rocky Memorial Dog Park
Address: Lakeville Highway and Casa Grande Road

PLEASANT HILL
Paso Nogal Dog Park
Address: Paso Nogal Road

PLEASANTON
Muirwood Community Dog Park
Address: 4701 Muirwood Drive

POWAY
Poway Community Dog Park
Address: 13094 Civic Center Drive
Hours: Open sunrise to sunset daily.

R
RANCHO SANTA MARGARITA
Rancho Santa Margarita Dog Park
Address: 24328 Antonio Parkway
Hours: Open sunrise to sunset.

REDDING

Benton Dog Park

Address: 1700 Airpark Drive

Hours: Open 6:00 am to 10:00 pm daily

REDONDO BEACH

Redondo Beach Dog Park

Address: Flagler Lane and 190th

Hours: Open sunrise to sunset. Closed Wednesdays until noon.

REDWOOD CITY

Shores Dog Park

Address: 1300-1400 Radio Road

Hours: Open sunrise to sunset.

RIO LINDA

Armand Nadeau Dog Park

Address: 810 Oak Lane

RIVERSIDE

Carlson Dog Park
Address: Mission Inn Avenue and Indian Hill Road

Pat Merritt Dog Park
Address: Limonite Frontage Road
Phone: 951-715-3440

Riverwalk Dog Park
Address: Pierce Street and Collett Avenue
Phone: 951-358-7387
Hours: Open 9:00 am to 9:00 pm daily.

ROSEVILLE

Bear Dog Park
Address: 1575 Pleasant Grove Boulevard
Hours: Closed Tuesday mornings from 6:00 am to 10:00 am

Marco Dog Park
Address: 1800 Sierra Gardens Drive
Hours: Closed Wednesday from dawn until 3:30 pm.

William "Bill" Hughes Dog Park
Address: 1600 Parkside Way
Hours: Closed Thursday 6:00 am to 10:00 am for maintenance.

S
SACRAMENTO
Bannon Creek Dog Park
Address: 2780 Azevedo Drive
Hours: Open 5:00 am to 10:00 pm daily.

Glenbrook Dog Park
Address: 8500 La Riviera Drive

Granite Dog Park
Address: 8200 Ramona Avenue
Hours: Open 5:00 am to 10:00 pm daily.

Howe Avenue Dog Park
Address: 2201 Cottage Way

Jacinto Creek Dog Park
Address: 8600 West Stockton Boulevard

North Natomas Regional Dog Park
Address: 2501 New Market Drive

Partner Dog Park
Address: 5699 South Land Park Drive
Hours: Open 5:00 am to 10:00 pm daily.

Regency Community Dog Park
Address: 5500 Honor Parkway

Sutter's Landing Dog Park
Address: 20 28th Street

Tanzanite Community Dog Park
Address: 2220 Tanzanite Way

WEST SACRAMENTO
Sam Combs Dog Park
Address: 205 Stone Boulevard

SAN BERNARDINO
Wildwood Dog Park
Address: 536 East 40th Street
Hours: Open 6:30 am to 10:30 pm daily.

SAN BRUNO

Commodore Park and Dog Exercise Area

Address: Commodore and Cherry Avenue

SAN CLEMENTE

San Clemente Dog Park

Address: 301 Avenida La Pata

Hours: Open sunrise to sunset.

SAN DIEGO

Capehart Dog Park

Address: Felspar and Soledad Mountain Road

Hours: Open 24 hours.

Doyle Community Dog Park

Address: 8175 Regents Road

Hours: Open 24 hours.

Dusty Rhodes Dog Park
Address: Sunset Cliffs Boulevard

Kearney Mesa Community Dog Park
Address: 3170 Armstrong Street
Hours: Open 6:30 am to 10:00 pm daily.

Nate's Point
Address: Sixth Avenue

Nobel Dog Park
Address: 8820 Judicial Drive

Rancho Bernardo Dog Park
Address: 18448 West Bernardo Drive

Rancho Panasquitos Park
Address: Salmon River Road
Hours: Open 24 hours.

Torrey Highlands Dog Park
Address: Landsdale Drive

SAN DIMAS

San Dimas Dog Park
Address: 301 Horsethief Canyon Road
Hours: Open sunrise to sunset. Closed Wednesday 1:00 pm to 3:00 pm.

SAN FRANCISCO

Golden Gate Dog Park
Address: 38th and Fulton Street

Eureka Valley Dog Park
Address: 18th Street and Collingwood
Hours: Open 6:00 am to 10:00 pm daily.

Mission Creek Dog Park
Address: 485 Berry Street
Hours: Open 6:00 am to 10:00 pm daily.

Upper Noe Dog Park
Address: 30th Street

Walter Haas Dog Park
Address: Diamond Heights and Addison

St. Mary's Dog Park
Address: 95 Justin Drive

SAN JOSE
Butcher Dog Park
Address: Camden Avenue

Delmas Dog Park
Address: Delmas and Park Avenue

Fontana Dog Park
Address: Golden Oak and Paseo Pueblo

Hellyer Dog Park
Address: Hellyer Avenue
Hours: Closed Wednesdays.

Miyuki Dog Park
Address: Miyuki Drive

Ryland Dog Park
Address: San Pedro

Selma Olinder Dog Park
Address: 18th and Williams

Watson Dog Park
Address: East Jackson and 22nd Street

Saratoga Creek Dog Park
Address: Graves Avenue
Hours: Open sunrise to sunset.

SAN LORENZO
San Lorenzo Dog Park
Address: 1970 Via Buena Vista
Phone: 510-881-6700

SAN LUIS OBISPO
El Chorro Regional Dog Park
Address: Highway 1 at Dairy Creek Road

SAN MATEO
Seal Point Dog Park
Address: 1801 East 3rd Avenue

SAN MARCOS

Montiel Park Dog Run
Address: Rancho Santa Fe Road and Linda Vista Drive
Phone: 760-744-1050

San Elijo Dog Park
Address: San Elijo Road and Elfin Forest Road
Phone: 760-744-1050

SAN RAMON

Del Mar Dog Park
Address: Del Mar at Pine Valley Road

Memorial Dog Park
Address: Bollinger Canyon Road

SANTA CLARA

Reed Street Dog Park

Address: 888 Reed Street

Hours: Open sunrise to sunset. Closed Thursdays.

SANTA CLARITA

Central Bark Dog Park

Address: 27150 Bouquet Canyon Road

Hours: Open sunrise to sunset.

SANTA MARIA

WOOF PAC Dog Park

Address: 300 Goodwin Road

Hours: Open 8:00 am to sunset.

SANTA MONICA

Airport Dog Park

Address: 3201 Airport Avenue

Phone: 310-458-8974

Joslyn Dog Park
Address: 633 Kensington Road
Hours: Open 6:00 am to 11:00 pm daily.

Memorial Dog Park
Address: 1401 Olympic Boulevard
Phone: 310-458-8974
Hours: Open 6:00 am to 11:00 pm daily.

Pacific Street Dog Park
Address: 145 Pacific Street
Hours: Open 6:00 am to 11:00 pm daily.

SANTA ROSA
DeTurk Round Barn Dog Park
Address: 819 Donahue Street

Doyle Community Dog Park
Address: 700 Doyle Park Drive

Galvin Community Dog Park
Address: 3330 Yulupa Avenue

Northwest Community Dog Park
Address: 2620 West Steele Lane

Rincon Valley Community Dog Park
Address: 5108 Badger Road

SAUSILITO
Sausilito Dog Park
Address: 3001 Bridgeway Avenue
Phone: 415-846-8323
Hours: Open sunrise to sunset daily.

Remington Dog Park
Address: Bridgeway and Ebbtide

SIERRA MADRE

Sierra Vista Dog Park

Address: 611 East Sierra Madre Boulevard

FYI: This dog park has an application process with the city.

Fees: $25.00 annually or $5.00 daily.

SIMI VALLEY

Simi Dog Park

Address: 2251 Lost Canyons Drive

STOCKTON

Barkleyville Dog Park

Address: Feather River Drive

Hours: Open sunrise to sunset. Closed Thursday mornings for maintenance.

STUDIO CITY

Laurel Canyon Dog Park
Address: 8260 Mulholland Drive
Phone: 818-769-4415
Hours: Open 24 hours.

SUNNYVALE

Las Palmas Dog Park
Address: 850 Russett Drive
Hours: Open 8:00 am to 8:00 pm daily.

T

TEHACHAPI/GOLDEN HILLS

Meadowbrook Dog Park
Address: Westwood Boulevard and Red Apple
Hours: Open sunrise to sunset.

TEMECULA
Redhawk Community Dog Park
Address: 44747 Redhawk Parkway
Phone: 951-694-6444

THOUSAND OAKS
Conejo Creek Dog Park
Address: 1350 Avenida de las Flores
Hours: Open 7:00 am to 8:30 pm. Closed Thursday 7:00 am to 9:00 am and all day every third Thursday of the month.

TRACY
El Pescadero Dog Park
Address: Tracy Boulevard and Kavanagh Avenue

TURLOCK
Sunnyview Dog Park
Address: 500 South Berkeley Avenue

U

UNION CITY

Drigon Dog Park

Address: Seventh Street and Mission Boulevard

Phone: 510-471-3232

Hours: Open 6:00 am to 10:00 pm. Closed Mondays and wet weather.

V

VACAVILLE

Janine Jordan Dog Park

Address: Riviera Road

VALEJO

Wardlaw Dog Park

Address: 1805 Ascot Parkway

Phone: 707-704-6167

VENICE

Westminster Dog Park

Address: 1234 Pacific Avenue

Phone: 310-301-1550

Hours: Open 5:00 am to 10:30 pm daily.

W

WALNUT CREEK

Wag World Dog Park

Address: 301 North San Carlos Drive

Hours: Open 8:00 am to sunset daily.

WATSONVILLE

Watsonville Dog Park

Address: 757 Green Valley Road

WOODLAND

Woodland Dog Park

Address: 2001 East Street and Road 24A

Y

YUBA CITY

Yuba Sutter Dog Park

Address: 2050 Wild River Drive

Hours: Open sunrise to sunset.

COLORADO

A

ARVADA

West Arvada Dog Park

Address: 17975 West 64th Parkway

Hours: Open sunrise to sunset.

AURORA

Grandview Dog Park

Address: 17500 East Quincy Avenue

Hours: Open sunrise to sunset.

B

BOULDER

East Boulder Dog Park

Address: 5660 Sioux Drive

Hours: Open sunrise to sunset.

Foothill Community Dog Park
Address: Cherry Street
Hours: Open sunrise to sunset.

BRIGHTON
Happy Trails Dog Park
Address: 1111 Judicial Center Drive
Phone: 303-655-2049
Hours: Open sunrise to sunset daily.

BROOMFIELD
Broomfield County Commons Dog Park
Address: Sheridan Boulevard and 13th

C
CASTLE ROCK
Fairgrounds Regional Park
Address: 1001 Plum Creek Parkway
Phone: 303-660-7495
Hours: Open sunrise to sunset daily.

Glendale Farm Open Space
Address: 800 Oak Lane
Phone: 303-660-7495
Hours: Open sunrise to sunset daily.

COLORADO SPRINGS
Bear Creek Dog Park
Address: 21st Street and Rio Grande
Phone: 719-520-7529

Cheyenne Meadows Dog Park
Address: Canoe Creek and Charmwood

Palmer Dog Park
Address: 3650 Maizeland Road

Rampart Dog Park
Address: 8270 Lexington Drive and Union

CONIFER

Beaver Ranch Dog Park

Address: 11369 Foxton Road

Hours: Open sunrise to sunset daily.

D

DENVER

Berkeley Dog Park

Address: 4801 West 46th

Phone: 720-913-0696

Fuller Dog Park

Address: 1600 East 29th

Phone: 720-913-0696

Green Valley Ranch East Park Off Leash Dog Area

Address: Jebel and East 45th

Phone: 720-913-0696

Hours: Open 5:00 am to 11:00 pm daily.

Jason Street Dog Park
Address: 978 South Jason Street
Hours: Open sunrise to sunset.

Stapleton Dog Park
Address: 2005 Spruce Street
Phone: 720-913-0696

E
ENGLEWOOD
Englewood Canine Corral Dog Park
Address: 4848 South Windermere Street
Phone: 303-762-2300

EVANS
Freedom Dog Park
Address: 2095 42nd Street
Hours: Open sunrise to sunset.

EVERGREEN

Elk Meadow Open Space Bark Dog Park
Address: Stagecoach Boulevard
Phone: 303-271-5925

F
FIRESTONE

Asik's Meadow Dog Park
Address: Saint Vrain Ranch Boulevard

Rough and Ready Dog Park
Address: 21st and Alpine

Stephen Day Dog Park
Address: 1340 Deerwood

FORT COLLINS

Fossil Creek Dog Park
Address: 5821 South Lemay Avenue

Soft Gold Dog Park
Address: 520 Hickory Street

Spring Canyon Dog Park
Address: West Horsetooth Road

G

GOLDEN

Golden Dog Park
Address: 4471 Salvia Street
Phone: 303-384-8100

Homer's Run Dog Park
Address: 17651 West 10th Avenue
Phone: 303-384-8100
Hours: Open 5:00 am to 10:00 pm daily.

H

HIGHLAND RANCH

Digger's Dog Park

Address: 3385 Asterbrook Circle

Phone: 303-791-2710

Hours: Open 7:00 am to sunset daily.

Fido's Field

Address: 1042 Riddlewood Drive

Phone: 303-791-2710

Hours: Open 7:00 am to sunset daily.

Glendale Farm Open Space Dog Park

Address: Near Surry Ridge and East of I-25

Hound Hill Dog Park

Address: 9651 South University Boulevard

Phone: 303-791-2710

Hours: Open 7:00 am to sunset daily.

Rover's Run Dog Park
Address: 9250 South Foothills Canyon Boulevard
Phone: 303-791-2710
Hours: Open 7:00 am to sunset daily.

L
LAFAYETTE
The Great Bark Dog Park
Address: 597 North 119th Street
Hours: Open sunrise to sunset.

LAKEWOOD
Forsberg/ Iron Spring Dog Park
Address: 15900 West Alameda Parkway

LITTLETON
David A. Lorenz Regional Dog Park
Address: 8560 South Colorado Boulevard

LONGMONT

Blue Skies Dog Park
Address: 1520 Mountain Drive

Dog Park #1
Address: Francis and 21st Street

Dog Park #2
Address: Airport Road and Saint Vrain Road

LOUISVILLE

Community Park Dog Park
Address: 955 Bella Vista Drive
Phone: 303-335-4735
Hours: Open sunrise to sunset daily.

N

NORTH GLENN

Waggin Tails Dog Park

Address: 10620 Irma Drive

Phone: 303-450-8718

Hours: Open sunrise to sunset.

P

PARKER

Bayou Gulch Regional Dog Park

Address: 7530 Fox Sparrow Road

Phone: 303-660-7400

W

WESTMINSTER

Big Dry Creek Dog Park

Address: 1700 West 128th Avenue

Westminster Dog Park

Address: 1051 North Simms Street

Phone: 303-430-2400

Hours: Open sunrise to sunset daily.

WINDSOR

Poudre Dog Park

Address: 1050 Larch Drive

HAWAII

H

HONOLULU

Bark Park

Address: Diamond Head Road and 18th Avenue

Hours: Open during daylight hours.

Hawaii Kai Dog Park

Address: Keahole Street

Phone: 808-396-5225

McInerny Dog Park

Address: 2700 Waialae Avenue

Phone: 808- 946-2187

Hours: Open 11:00 am to 7:00 pm Monday through Friday and 10:00 am to 4:00 pm Saturday, Sunday and Holidays.

Moanalua Dog Park

Address: Moanalua Park Road

Hours: Open sunrise to sunset. Closed Tuesday until noon for maintenance.

L

LIHUE

Freddie's Dog Park

Address: 3-825 Kaumualii Highway

Hours: Open 8:00 am to 6:00 pm Tuesday through Friday and 8:00 am to 6:00 pm Saturday through Monday.

IDAHO

B

BOISE

Morris Hill Dog Park

Address: 10 Roosevelt Street

Hours: Open sunrise to sunset daily.

M

MOSCOW

Moscow Dog Park

Address: 2019 White Avenue

Hours: Open sunrise to sunset daily.

N

NAMPA

Nampa Dog Park

Address: Second street south and East Amity Avenue

Hours: Open sunrise to sunset.

S

STATE LINE

Gateway Dog Park

Address: Milepost 1 of Centennial Trail

Hours: Open sunrise to sunset.

MONTANA

B

BOZEMAN

Canine Beach Dog Park
Address: 700-550 North Fowler
Hours: Open 8:00 am to 10:00 pm daily.

Dog Park at Softball Complex
Address: 710-799 Highland Boulevard
Hours: Open 8:00 am to 10:00 pm daily.

G

GREAT FALLS

The Pacific Steel & Recycling Dog Park
Address: 800 River Drive North

M

MISSOULA

Jacob's Island

Address: Van Buren and 5th

Hours: Open 6:00 am to 11:00 pm daily.

W

WHITEFISH

Hugh Rogers Wag Dog Park

Address: 2nd Street Armory Park complex.

NEVADA

H

HENDERSON

Acacia Dog Park

Address: 30 Casa Del Fuego Street

Hours: Open 6:00 am to midnight daily.

Cactus Wren Dog Park

Address: 2900 Ivanpah Drive

Hours: Open 6:00 am to midnight daily.

Dos Escuelas Dog Park

Address: 1 Golden View Drive

Hours: Open 6:00 am to midnight daily.

Esselmont Dog Park

Address: 2725 Anthem Highlands Drive

Hours: Open 6:00 am to midnight daily.

Paseo Vista Dog Park
Address: 2505 Paseo Verde Parkway
Hours: Open 6:00 am to midnight daily.

L
LAS VEGAS
All American Dog Park
Address: 121 East Sunset Road
Phone: 702-317-7777

Barkin Basin Dog Park
Address: Alexander Road and Tenaya Way
Phone: 702-229-6297

Centennial Hills Dog Park
Address: Elkhorn and Buffalo Drive
Phone: 702-229-6297

Children's Memorial Dog Park
Address: 6601 West Gowan Road
Phone: 702-229-6718

Desert Breeze Dog Run
Address: 8425 West Spring Mountain Road

Desert Inn Dog Park
Address: 3570 Vista del Monte
Phone: 702- 455-8200

Dog Fancier's Park
Address: 5800 East Flamingo Road
Phone: 702-455-8200

Jaycee Dog Park
Address: East Saint Louis Avenue and Eastern Avenue
Phone: 702-229-6718

Kellogg-Zaher Sports Complex Dog Park
Address: 7901 West Washington Avenue
Phone: 702-229-6297

Lorenzi Dog Park
Address: 3075 West Washington Avenue
Phone: 702-229-4867

Molasky Park Dog Run
Address: 1065 East Twain Avenue
Phone: 702-455-8200

Police Memorial Dog Park
Address: Metro Academy Way and Cheyenne Avenue
Phone: 702-229-6297

Shadow Rock Dog Park
Address: 2650 Los Feliz on Sunrise Mountain
Phone: 702-455-8200

Silverado Ranch Dog Park
Address: 9855 South Gillespie
Phone: 702-455-8200

Sunset Dog Park
Address: 2601 East Sunset Road
Phone: 702-455-8200

Woofter Dog Park
Address: Rock Springs and Vegas Drive
Phone: 702-633-1171

R

RENO

Link Piazzo Dog Park
Address: 4740 Parkway Drive
Phone: 775-823-6501

Rancho San Rafael Regional Dog Park
Address: 1595 North Sierra Street
Phone: 775-785-4512

Sparks Marina Park
Address 300 Howard Drive
Phone: 775-353-2376

Virginia Lake Dog Park
Address: Lakeside Drive
Phone: 775-334-2099

Whitaker Dog Park
Address: 550 University Terrace
Phone: 775-334-2099

NEW MEXICO

A

ALAMOGORDO
Bark Park Dog Park
Address: Fairgrounds Road

ALBUQUEQUE
Santa Fe Village Dog Park
Address: 5700 Bogart Street NW
Phone: 505-768-1975

Coronado Dog Park
Address: 301 McKnight Avenue NW
Phone: 505-768-1975

Los Altos Dog Park
Address: 821 Eubank Boulevard NE
Phone: 505-768-1975

Tom Bolack Urban Forest Dog Park
Address: Haines Avenue
Phone: 505-873-6620

USS Bullhead Dog Park
Address: 1606 San Pedro SE
Phone: 505-768-1975

Rio Grande Triangle Dog Park
Address: Iron Avenue
Phone: 505-873-6620

Roosevelt Park Dog Park
Address: Hazeldine Avenue

G
GALLUP
Highway 40 Rest Stop Dog Park

Address: Highway 40 heading east

L
LAS CRUCES
Las Cruces Dog Park

Address: Hermosa Street in the Hadley Complex

Hours: Open 6:00 am to dusk daily.

R
RIO RANCHO
Rainbow Dog Park

Address: Southern Boulevard at Atlantic

S
SANTA FE
Santa Fe Animal Shelter Dog Park
Address: 100 Caja del Rio Road
Phone: 505-983-4309

W
WHITE ROCK
Dog Haven at Overlook Park
Address: Overlook Drive
Phone: 505-327-5221

OREGON

A

ASHLAND

Ashland Dog Park

Address: Nevada and Helman Streets

B

BEAVERTON

Hazeldale Dog Park

Address: SW 192nd and Farmington Road

BEND
Big Sky Youth Sports Complex Dog Park

Address: 21690 Neff Road

C

COQUILLE

Coquille Dog Park

Address: East 5th Street Park

Phone: 541-396-3132

D

DALLAS

Central Bark

Address: 920 SE Juniper Street

E

EUGENE

Alton Baker Dog Park

Address: Leo Harris Parkway

Phone: 541-682-4800

Amazon Dog Park
Address: Amazon Parkway
Phone: 541-682-4800

Candlelight Dog Park
Address: Royal Avenue
Phone: 541-682-4800

Morse Ranch Dog Park
Address: 595 Crest Drive
Phone: 541-682-4800

H

HILLSBORO

Hondo Dog Park
Address: 4499 NW 229th Street

L

LAKE OSWEGO

Luscher Farm Dog Park

Address: Stafford Road

Hours: Open sunrise to sunset.

M

MEDFORD

Bear Creek Dog Park

Address: Highland Drive

Phone: 541-774-2400

MILWAUKIE

North Clackamas Dog Park

Address: 5440 SE Kellog Creek Drive

Phone: 503-794-8002

P

PORTLAND

Chimney Dog Park
Address: 9360 North Columbia Boulevard
Phone: 503-823-7529

East Delta Dog Park
Address: North Union Court
Phone: 503-823-7529

Normandale Dog Park
Address: NE 57th Avenue at Halsey Street
Phone: 503-823-7529

Brentwood Dog Park
Address: 60th Street and Duke
Phone: 503- 823-7529

Gabriel Dog Park
Address: SW 45th Avenue and Vermont
Phone: 503-823-7529

R

ROSEBERG

Happy Tails Dog Park

Address: 100 SE Templin

T

TIGARD

Ash Street Dog Park

Address: 12770 SW Ash Avenue

Phone: 503-639-4171

Potso Dog Park

Address: Wall Street at Hunziker Street

Phone: 503-639-4171

Summer Lake Dog Park

Address: 11450 SW Winterlake Drive

Phone: 503-639-4171

W
WEST LINN
Mary S. Young Dog Park

Address: Highway 43

Phone: 503-557-4700

WILSONVILLE
Memorial Park Off Leash Dog Park

Address: 8100 SW Wilsonville Road

Phone: 503-682-3727

UTAH

P

PARK CITY

Trailside Dog Park
Address: 5715 Trailside Drive

Park City Dog Park
Address: Round Valley Drive and Gilmore Way

R

ROY

Roy City Dog Park
Address: 5700 South 3260 West

S
SALT LAKE CITY

Jordan Dog Park
Address: 1060 South 900 West
Phone: 801-972-7800

Herman Frank's Park
Address: 700 East 1300 South

Lindsey Gardens
Address: 9th Avenue and M Street
Phone: 901-972-7800

S
SANDY

Sandy City Dog Park
Address: 9980 South 300 East
Phone: 801-568-2900

Quail Hollow Dog Park
Address: 9100 South 2900 East

SOUTH OGDEN
South Ogden Dog Park

Address: 4150 South Palmer Drive

Hours: Open sunrise to sunset. Closed November 1 through March 31 for winter.

ST GEORGE
JC Snow Park

Address: 900 South 400 East

T
TAYLORSVILLE
Millrace Dog Park

Address: 1200 West 5400 South

Phone: 801-963-5400

W

WEST JORDAN

West Jordan Off Leash Dog Park

Address: 5982 West New Bingham Highway

WASHINGTON

A
ANACORTES
Ace of Hearts Rotary Dog Park

Address: 38th and H Avenues

B
BELLEVUE
Robinswood Animal Corral

Address: 2430 148th Avenue SE

BELLINGHAM

Lake Padden Dog Park

Address: 4882 Samish Way

BOTHELL

Tambark Dog Park

Address: 17217 35th Avenue SE

BRUSH PRAIRIE

Brush Prairie Dog Park

Address: 149th Street

Hours: Open 7:00 am to dusk.

C

CENTRALIA

Fort Borst Dog Park

Address: 902 Johnston

Hours: Open dawn to dusk.

E

EBEY ISLAND

Ebey Island Dog Park

Address: 55th Avenue SE

EVERETT

Lowell Dog Park

Address: 4605 South 3rd Avenue

Hours: Open 6:00 am to 10:00 pm daily.

F

FEDERAL WAY

French Lake Dog Park

Address: 31531 1st Avenue South

Hours: Open 7:00 am to 9:00 pm, May through August and 7:00 am to dusk September through April.

FRIDAY HARBOR

Eddie and Friends Dog Park

Address: Mullis Street

Hours: Open 7:00 am to dusk daily.

I

ISSAQUAH HIGHLANDS

Issaquah Highlands Bark Park

Address: 25th and Natalie Way

K

KITSAP

Bandix Dog Park

Address: Bandix Road SE at Burley- Olalla Road

L

LAKEWOOD

Fort Steilacoom Dog Park

Address: 8714-87th Avenue SW

LONGVIEW

Longview Dog Park

Address: 40 Tennant Way

Hours: Open sunrise to sunset.

M

MARYSVILLE

Strawberry Fields Dog Park

Address: 6100 152nd Street

Phone: 360-363-8400

MERCER ISLAND

Luther Burbank Dog Park

Address: 2040 84th Avenue SE

Hours: Open 6:00 am to 10:00 pm daily.

MONROE

Wiggley Field

Address: 413 Sky River Parkway

Phone: 360-863-4559

MOUNT VERNON

Bakerview Park

Address: 3101 East Fir Street

MOUNTLAKE TERRACE

Mountlake Terrace Dog Park

Address: 53rd Avenue West and 228th Street SW

Hours: Open sunrise to sunset.

O

ORCAS ISLAND

Orcas Island Dog Park

Address: Mount Baker and North Beach Roads

P

POULSBO

Raab Dog Park

Address: 18349 Caldart Avenue

R

REDMOND

Marymoor Park Off Leash Dog Area

Address: 6046 West Lake Sammamish Parkway NE

Phone: 206-205-3661

RENTON

Cedar River Off Leash Dog Park

Address: Near South 3rd Street near Cedar River Trail

RUSTON

Rust Dog Park

Address: Commercial Street

S

SAMMAMISH

Beaver Lake Dog Park

Address: 244th Avenue

SEATTLE

Blue Dog Pond

Address: 1400 Martin Luther King Jr Way South

Dr. Jose Rizal Dog Park

Address: 1008 12th Avenue South

Genesee Dog Park
Address: 4316 South Genesee Street

Golden Garden Dog Park
Address: 8498 Seaview Place NW

I-5 Colonnade Park
Address: Beneath I-5, South of East Howe Street

North Acres Dog Park
Address: 12718 1st Avenue NE

Plymouth Pillars Dog Park
Address: Boren Avenue and Pike Street

Regrade Dog Park
Address: 2251 3rd Avenue

Warren G. Magnuson Dog Park
Address: 7400 Sand Point Way NE

Westcrest Dog Park

Address: 9000 8th Avenue SW

Woodland Dog Park

Address: Aurora Avenue North and North 59th Street

SEQUIM

Sequim Dog Park

Address: 202 North Blake Road

SNOHOMISH

Willis Tucker Dog Park

Address: 6705 Puget Park Drive

Hours: Open 7:00 am to dusk daily.

T

TACOMA

Rogers Dog Park

Address: East 34th Street and East L Street

V

VANCOUVER

Dakota Memorial Dog Park
Address: NE 18th Street between NE 164th Avenue and 172nd Avenue
Phone: 360-619-1123

Ross Dog Park
Address: NE Ross Street and NE 18th Street

W

WALLA WALLA

Walla Walla Dog Park
Address: Dalles Military Road near Myra Road
Hours: Open 5:00 am to 11:00 pm daily.

WHIDBEY ISLAND

Clover Valley Dog Park
Address: Christian Road

Marguerite Brons Memorial Dog Park
Address: Bayview Road

Oak Harbor Dog Park
Address: Technical Drive

Patmore Pit Dog Park
Address: Patmore Road

Y
YAKIMA
Norman and Nellie Byrd Dog Park
Address: East R Street

WYOMING

C
CHEYENNE
Cheyenne Community Dog Park
Address: 800 Southwest

ARKANSAS

F

FAYETVILLE

Animal Services Facility

Address: 1640 South Armstrong

Phone: 479-444-3456

Hours: Open 8:00 am to dusk daily, except holidays.

FORT SMITH

Fort Smith Dog Park

Address: Corner of Massard Road and Louisville Street

J

JACKSONVILLE

Dogwood Park

Address: 7407 Salisbury Road South

Hours: For members, dawn until 10:00 pm.

Hours: For non-members, Saturday 10:00 am to 5:00 pm and Sunday noon to 5:00 pm.

L

LITTLE ROCK

Paws Park at Murray Park
Address: Rebsamen Park Road
Phone: 501-371-4770

Burns Dog Park
Address: I-40 Exit # 150

M

MAUMELLE

4 Paws Park
Address: Hyman Drive
Hours: Open sunrise to sunset.

Murphy Dog Park
Address: Nursery Road

ILLINOIS

A

ADDISON
Du Page County Dog Training Area
Address: Swift Road

AURORA
Paws In The Park at Lincoln Park
Address: South Harrison Avenue and Lakewood
Phone: 630-897-0516
Fees: $15.00 for residents and $30.00 for non residents.

C

CHAMPAIGN
Champaign Dog Park
Address: Windsor Road
Fees: $40.00 annually for resident or $60.00 annually for non resident.

CHICAGO

Challenger Play Lot Dog Park
Address: 1100 West Irving Park Road
Phone: 312-742-7529
Fees: $5.00 yearly registration.

Churchill Field Play Lot Dog Park
Address: 1825 North Damen Avenue
Phone: 312-742-7529
Fees: $5.00 yearly registration.

Coliseum Dog Park
Address: 1466 South Wabash Avenue
Phone: 312-742-7529
Fees: $5.00 yearly registration.

Grant Dog Park
Address: Columbus Drive and 9th Street
Phone: 312-742-7529
Fees: $5.00 yearly registration.

Hamlin Dog Park
Address: 3035 North Hoyne Avenue
Phone: 312-742-7529
Fees: $5.00 yearly registration.

Margate Dog Park
Address: 4921 North Marine Drive
Phone: 312-742-7529
Fees: $5.00 yearly registration.

Noethling Park Dog Park
Address: 2645 North Sheffield Avenue
Phone: 312-742-7529
Fees: $5.00 yearly registration.

Park No 511
Address: 630 Kingsbury

Park No 546
Address: 450 East Benton Place

Park No 551
Address: 353 North Des Plaines

River Park Dog Park
Address: 5100 North Francisco Avenue
Phone: 312-742-7529
Fees: $5.00 yearly registration.

Walsh Park Dog Park
Address: 1722 North Ashland Avenue
Phone: 312-742-7529
Fees: $5.00 yearly registration.

Wicker Park Dog Park
Address: 1425 North Damen Avenue
Phone: 312-742-7529
Fees: $5.00 yearly registration.

CRYSTAL LAKE

Hound Town Dog Park

Address: Route 176

Phone: 815-459-0680

Fees for non residents: $45.00 fee for dog + $10.00 for each additional dog. Senior citizen rate is $30.00 + $5.00 each additional dog.

Fees for residents: $30.00 fee for dog + $6.00 for each additional dog. Senior citizen rate is half price.

D

DEER FIELD

Jaycees Park

Address: 1050 Wilmott Road

Phone: 847-945-0650

DES PLAINS

E.J. Beck Lake

Address: 8939A Robin Drive

Phone: 708-771-1036

Hours: Open sunrise to sunset.

Fees: Permit required. $50.00 per dog.

F

FRANKFORT

Frankfort Bark Park

Address: Laraway and 80th Avenue South

Phone: 815-469-9400

Fees: $50.00 annual fee and $ 10.00 key card fee.

FREEPORT

Friends Forever Dog Park

Address: 966 Rudy Road

Hours: Open sunrise to sunset.

Fees: $30.00 annually or $2.00 day pass.

G

GLENVIEW

Community Bark West

Address: 1001 Zenith Drive

Hours: Open sunrise to sunset. Closed Tuesday and Wednesday from 8:30 to 11:30 a.m.

Fees: $50.00 residents and $100 non residents.

H
HIGHLAND PARK

Highland Park Golf Learning Center Dog Park
Address: 2205 Skokie Valley Road
Phone: 847-579-4087
Fees: $40.00 annually residents or $140 annually for non residents.

Moraine Dog Beach and Park
Address: 2501 Sheridan Road
Phone: 847-579-4087
Hours: Open dawn to dusk- April 1 through October 31st. Closed November through March.
Fees: $40.00 annually residents or $140 annually for non residents.

HOFFMAN ESTATES

Willow Dog Park

Address: 3600 Lexington Drive

Hours: Open 8:00 am to sunset.

Fees: $25.00 annually for residents and $40.00 for non residents.

HOMER GLEN

Messenger Marsh Dog Park

Address: South Bell Road

Fees: $25.00 annually for residents and $50.00 for non residents.

HOMEWOOD

Rover's Run Dog Park

Address: 191st Street and Center Avenue

Hours: Open sunrise to sunset.

Fees: $15.00 annually for residents and $25.00 for non residents.

L

LAKE FOREST

Prairie Wolf Slough Dog Park

Address: South Waukegan Road

Phone: 847-367-6640

Fees: $44.00 annually for residents and $120.00 for non residents. Daily permits available on location. $5.00 for residents and $10.00 for non residents.

LAKE VILLA

Duck Farm Dog Park

Address: Grand Avenue (Route 132)

Phone: 847- 367-6640

Hours: Open 6:30 am to sunset. Closed the first and third Wednesday until 11:00 am for mowing.

LAKE IN THE HILLS

Lake In The Hills Dog Park

Address: 9027 Haligus Road

Hours: Open dawn to 9:00 pm.

Fees: $40.00 for residents and $60.00 for non residents.

LIBERTYVILLE

Independence Grove Dog Park

Address: Milwaukee Avenue (Route 21)

Phone: 847-367-6640

Hours: Open 6:30 am to sunset. Closed the first and third Tuesday until 11:00 am for maintenance.

Fees: $44.00 annually for residents and $120.00 for non residents.

M

MACOMB

Patton Dog Park

Address: Grant Street and Ward Street

Phone: 309-833-4562

Hours: Open daylight hours.

MORTON

Oakwood Dog Park

Address: North Main Street

N

NAPERVILLE

Green Valley Forest Preserve Dog Park

Address: Greene Road

Phone: 630-933-7248

Hours: Open one hour after sunrise to one hour after sunset.

Fees: $40.00 annually for residents and $150.00 for non residents. Day permits available.

Springbrook Prairie Forest Reserve Dog Park
Address: 83rd Street
Phone: 630-933-7248
Hours: Open one hour after sunrise to one hour after sunset.
Fees: $40.00 annually for residents and $150.00 for non residents. Day permits available.

Whalon Lake Dog Park
Address: Royce Road
Fees: $25.00 per dog for residents and $50.00 for non residents annually or a $3.00 day pass.

NORMAL
Maxwell Dog Park
Address: Gregory Street

O

OAK BROOK

Mayslake Forest Preserve Dog Park

Address: St. Paschal's Drive

Phone: 630-933-7248

Hours: Open one hour after sunrise to one hour after sunset.

Fees: $40.00 annually for residents of the county and $150.00 for non residents. Day permits available.

O'FALLON

Rock Springs Dog Park

Address: End of East 3rd street off South 7 Hills Road

OAK PARK

Oak Park Dog Park

Address: Lake Street

Hours: Open sunrise to sunset.

Fees: $39.00 for the first dog and $5.00 for additional dogs.

P

PEKIN

Happy Tails Dog Park

Address: Court Street

PEORIA

Bradley Dog Park

Address: Park Road

R

ROCKFORD

Canine Corners Dog Park

Address: Central and Safford Road

Canine Corners Dog Park

Address: Lyford Road

Phone: 815-987-8800

Fees: $25.00 annually or $3.00 for a day pass.

S

SHOREWOOD

Hammel Woods Dog Park

Address: Black Road

Fees: $25.00 annually for residents and $50.00 for non residents.

U

URBANA

Urbana Dog Park

Address: 1501 East Perkins Road

Phone: 217-367-1544

Hours: Open sunrise to sunset.

Fees: $38.00 annually for residents and $76.00 for non residents. $6.00 day pass also available.

W

WARRENVILLE

Blackwell Forest Preserve Dog Park
Address: Mack Road
Phone: 630-933-7248
Hours: Open one hour after sunrise to one hour after sunset.
Fees: $40.00 annually for residents and $150.00 for non residents. Day permits available.

WAUCONDA

Lakewood Dog Park
Address: Fairfield Road
Phone: 847-367-6640
Fees: $44.00 annually for residents and $120.00 for non residents. Daily permits available on location.

IOWA

B

BETTENDORF

Crow Creek Dog Park

Address: 4800 North Devils Glen Road

C

CEDAR FALLS

Paw Park

Address: South Main and Highway 58 Overpass.

CEDAR RAPIDS

Cheyenne Park Off Leash Area

Address: Cedar Bend Lane Southwest

CLINTON

Prairie Pasture Dog Park

Address: 3900 North 3rd Street

Hours: Open 8:00 am to dusk.

D

DAVENPORT

CM Dog Training Center and Dog Park

Address: 8108 102 East Kimberly Road

Hours: Open dawn to dusk except rain days.

I

IOWA CITY

Thornberry Off Leash Dog Park

Address: West End of Foster Road

R

RUNNELLS

Rovers Ranch

Address: 200 SE 108th Street

Phone: 515-967-6768

S

SIOUX CITY

Lewis and Clark Dog Park

Address: 5201 Correctionville Road

W

WASHINGTON

Sunset Dog Park

Address: 915 West Main Street

Hours: Open 6:00 am to 10:00 pm.

WEST DES MOINES

Raccoon River Dog Park

Address: 2500 Grand Avenue

KANSAS

D

DE SOTO

Kill Creek Streamway Park
Address: 33460 West 95th Street

E

EMPORIA

Buck Fund Dog Park
Address: 2920 West 24th Avenue
Hours: Open sunrise to sunset.

G

GARDEN CITY

Garden City Dog Park
Address: Campus Drive and Fulton
Phone: 620-276-1200

H

HUTCHINSON

Hutchinson Dog Park

Address: 1501 South Severance Street

Hours: Open 5:00 am to midnight.

K

KANSAS CITY

Wyandotte County Lake Off Leash Area

Address: 91st Street and Leavenworth Road

Phone: 913-596-7077

Hours: Open 6:00 am to midnight.

L

LAWRENCE

Mutt Run Off Leash Dog Area

Address: 1330 East 902 Road

OLATHE

Heritage Park

Address: 159th and Pflumm Road

OVERLAND PARK

Thomas S. Stoll Memorial Park

Address: 12500 West 119th Street

S

SALINA

Salina Animal Shelter's Dog Park

Address: 329 North Second

Phone: 785-826-6535

Hours: Open 6:00 am to dark Monday through Friday. 8:00 am to 7:00 pm weekends. 9:00 am to 4:00 pm holidays.

SHAWNEE

Shawnee Mission Park

Address: 79th and Renner Road

T

TOPEKA

Hill's Bark Park

Address: 10th Street and Gage Boulevard

Hours: Open 6:00 am to 11:00 pm.

LOUISIANA

B

BATON ROUGE

Burbank Dog Park
Address: 12400 Burbank Drive
Hours: Open sunrise to sunset.

Forest Dog Park
Address: 13950 South Harrell's Ferry Road
Hours: Open sunrise to sunset.

Raising Cane's Dog Park
Address: 1442 City Park Avenue
Hours: Open sunrise to sunset.

L

LAFAYETTE

Lafayette Dog Park

Address: 1919 Johnston Street

Hours: Closed Thursday mornings until 3:00 pm.

LAKE CHARLES

Calcasieu Parish Animal Control Public Dog Park

Address: 5500-A Swift Plant Road

Hours: Open sunrise to sunset.

M

METAIRIE

Bonnabel Boat Launch Dog Park

Address: 1599 Bonnabel Boulevard

N
NEW ORLEANS
NOLA City Bark
Address: Zachary Taylor Drive, Diagonal Drive and Magnolia Drive

Z
ZACHARY
Zachary Community Dog Park
Address: 20055 Old Scenic Highway 964

MINNESOTA

B

BLOOMINGTON
Bloomington Dog Park
Address: 111th Street

BURNSVILLE
Alimagnet Dog Park
Address: 1200 Alimagnet Parkway
Phone: 952-895-4500
Hours: Open 5:00 am to 10:00pm.
Fees: $20.00 annually.

C

COON RAPIDS
Trackside Dog Park
Address: 10425 Hummingbird Street
Hours: Open sunrise to sunset.

CRYSTAL

Bassett Creek Dog Park
Address: 6001 32nd Avenue

Iron Horse Dog Park
Address: Jersey and 52nd Avenue

Lions Valley Place Dog Park
Address: 3224 Louisiana Avenue

Welcome Dog Park
Address: 4630 Welcome

D

DULUTH

Keene Creek Dog Park
Address: Grand Avenue and I-35
Hours: Open 8:00 am to 10:00 pm.

E

EDEN PRAIRIE

7171 Flying Cloud Drive
Phone: 952-949-8442
Hours: Open 6:00 am to 10:00 pm.

Bryant Lake Regional Dog Park
Address: 6400 Rowland Road
Phone: 763-559-9000
Fees: $30.00 annually or a $5.00 use fee at dog park.

Crestwood Park Hockey Rink Dog Park
Address: 9780 Dell Road
Phone: 952-949-8442
Hours: Open 6:00 am to 10:00 pm April through October. Closed November through March.

Edenvale Park Hockey Rink Dog Park
Address: 7200 Edenvale Boulevard
Phone: 952-949-8442
Hours: Open 6:00 am to 10:00 pm April through October. Closed November through March.

Homeward Hills Park Hockey Rink Dog Park
Address: 12000 Silverwood Drive
Phone: 952-949-8442
Hours: Open 6:00 am to 10:00 pm April through October. Closed November through March.

Nesbitt Preserve Park Hockey Rink Dog Park
Address: 8641 Center Way
Phone: 952-949-8442
Hours: Open 6:00 am to 10:00 pm April through October. Closed November through March.

Staring Lake Park Off Leash Area
Address: 13800 Pioneer Trail
Phone: 952-949-8442
Hours: Open 6:00 am to 10:00 pm. Closed December through March for cross country skiing.

E
ELK RIVER
Elk River Dog Park
Address: 1104 Lions Park Drive NW

EMPIRE
Dakota Woods Dog Park
Address: 16470 Blaine Avenue
Fees: $42.70

F

FRIDLEY

Locke Dog Park

Address: 450 71st Avenue NE

Hours: Open sunrise to sunset.

H

HIBBING

North Hibbing Dog Park

Address: 4th Avenue East and McKinley Street

M

MANKATO

Kiwanis Recreation Area Dog Park

Address: Highway 169

MAPLE GROVE

Elm Creek Reserve Dog Park

Address: Goose Lake Road and Elm Creek Road

Phone: 763-559-9000

Fees: $30.00 annual permit or a $5.00 day use fee at dog park.

MINNEAPOLIS

Gateway Dog Grounds

Address: 4th Avenue South between 10th and 11th Street South

Lake of The Isles Dog Park

Address: Lake of the Isles Parkway

Hours: Open 6:00 am to 10:00 pm.

Fees: $30.00 for altered dogs and $50.00 for unaltered dogs annually.

Loring Dog Park Grounds
Address: 1650 Harmon Place
Phone: 612-348-4250
Hours: Open 6:00 am to 10:00 pm.
Fees: $30.00 for altered dogs and $50.00 for unaltered dogs annually.

Minnehaha Falls Off Leash Dog Park
Address: 54th Street and Hiawatha Avenue
Phone: 612- 661-4800
Hours: Open 6:00 am to 10:00 pm.
Fees: $30.00 for altered dogs and $50.00 for unaltered dogs annually.

North Loop Dog Grounds
Address: 3rd Street North and 8th Avenue North

St Anthony Parkway Dog Park
Address: 700 Street Anthony Parkway
Hours: Open 6:00 am to 10:00 pm.
Fees: $30.00 for altered dogs and $50.00 for unaltered dogs annually.

N
NORTHFIELD
Northfield Dog Park
Address: Highway 3 near Highway 19

P
PRIOR LAKE
Cleary Lake Regional Dog Park
Address: Just north of 190th
Phone: 763-559-9000
Fees: $30.00 annually or $5.00 day use fee at the dog park.

R

ROCHESTER

Jean and Carl Frank NW Canine Park
Address: West side of West Circle Drive

ROCKFORD

Lake Sarah Regional Dog Park
Address: West Lake Sarah Drive
Phone: 763-559-9000
Fees: $30.00 annually or $5.00 day use fee at the dog park.

S

SOUTH ST. PAUL

Kaposia Landing Dog Park
Address: 800 Bryant Avenue
Hours: Open 8:00 am to 10:00 pm.
Fees: $20.00 annually.

ST LOUIS PARK

Carlson Dog Park

Address: 2541 Nevada Avenue

Hours: Open 7:00 am to 8:30 pm.

Fees: $25.00 annually for residents and $50.00 for non residents.

Dakota Dog Park

Address: 27th and Dakota Avenue

Hours: Open 7:00 am to 8:30 pm.

Fees: $25.00 annually for residents and $50.00 for non residents.

ST PAUL

Arlington/Arkwright Off Leash Dog Area

Address: Arlington and Arkwright

Hours: Open sunrise to 9:00 pm.

Battle Creek Regional Dog Park
Address: McKnight Road

V
VICTORIA
Carver Park Reserve Dog Park
Address: Park Drive and 73rd Street
Phone: 763-559-9000
Fees: $30.00 annually or a $5.00 day use permit.

W
WHITE BEAR
Otter Lake Regional Dog Park
Address: Otter Lake Road

WOODBURY
Dale Road Open Space Dog Park
Address: Dale Road

MISSISSIPPI

P

PETAL

Petal Dog Park

Address: Dawson Cut Off

S

STARKVILLE

Moncrief Dog Park

Address: Moncrief Park Street

Phone: 662-323-2294

Hours: Open dawn to 10:00 pm.

MISSOURI

A

ARNOLD

Paw Park

Address: Lakeside Drive

Phone: 636-282-6680

Hours: Open sunrise to sunset.

B

BLUE SPRINGS

Blue Springs Dog Park

Address: 20th Street off Jefferson

C

COLUMBIA

Twin Lakes Recreational Area Dog Park

Address: 2500 Chapel Hill Road

Garth Nature Area Dog Park
Address: 2799 North Garth

CREVE COEUR
Creve Coeur Dog Park
Address: 12301 Conway Road
Phone: 314-872-2510
Fees: $30.00 annually for residents and $80.00 for non residents.

F
FLORRISANT
Florrisant Dog Park
Address: Manion Park Drive
Hours: Open 8:00 am to 11:00 pm.
Fees: $30.00 annually for residents and $80.00 for non residents.

K

KANSAS CITY

Penn Valley Dog Park

Address: West 29th Street and Wyandotte

Hours: Open dawn to one hour after dusk.

Wayside Waifs Bark Park

Address: 3901 Martha Truman Road

Phone: 816-761-8151

Hours: Open 24 hours.

Fees: $120 annually, $17.50 monthly or $2.00 per day.

L

LEES SUMMIT

Happy Tails Dog Park

Address: 1251 SE Ranson Road

Hours: Open 6:00 am to 9:00 pm or sunset.

M

MARYLAND HEIGHT

Dogport Dog Park

Address: McKelvey Woods Court

Hours: Open sunrise to sunset.

Fees: $30.00 annually for residents of Maryland Heights and Bridgeton only.

N

NORTH JEFFERSON CITY

Address: 810 Sandstone Drive

Hours: 5:00 am to dark. Closed Monday 5:00 am to noon for maintenance and noon to dark.

Fees: $12.00 annual usage permit required.

S

SPRINGFIELD

Cruse Dog Park

Address: Grand and Catalpa Street

Phone: 417-864-1049

Hours: Open sunrise to sunset.

Fees: $25.00 annually or $10.00 day pass.

ST CHARLES

Du Sable Dog Park

Address: 2598 North Main Street

Hours: Open daylight to 10:00 pm.

ST LOUIS

John and Lucille Wendling Soulard Dog Park

Address: Emmett Street and South 10th Street

Hours: Open 6:00 am to 9:00 pm.

Fees: $50.00 annual donation requested.

Lister Dog Park
Address: North Taylor Avenue and Olive Street
Hours: Open 8:00 am to 9:00 pm Monday through Friday and 9:00 am to 10:00 pm weekends.
Fees: $45.00 annually.

Shaw Dog Park
Address: Cleveland and Thurman Avenues
Hours: Open 6:00 am to 10:00pm.
Fees: $25.00 for residents and $50.00 for non residents.

Southwest City Dog Park
Address: Jamieson Avenue and Hampton Avenue
Fees: $35.00 for residents and $60.00 for non residents.

Taylor Dog Park
Address: North Taylor Avenue and Maryland
Hours: Open 8:00 am to 9:00 pm Monday through Friday and 9:00 am to 10:00 pm weekends.
Fees: $45.00 annually.

Water Tower Dog Park
Address: South Grand Boulevard
Phone: 314-865-2374
Hours: Open 5:00am to 10:00 pm.

U
UNIVERSITY CITY
University City Dog Park
Address: Vernon Avenue and Pennsylvania Avenue
Hours: Open 5:30 am to 10:00 pm.

W

WENTZVILLE

Quail Ridge Dog Park

Address: Quail Ridge Parkway

Hours: Open sunrise to sunset.

Broemmelsiek Dog Park

Address: Wilson Road

NEBRASKA

B

BEATRICE

Beatrice Dog Park

Address: South 6th and Cole Street

BELLEVUE

Jewell Dog Park

Address: Franklin Street

H

HASTINGS

Hastings Dog Park

Address: East South Street

K

KEARNEY

Meadowlark North Dog Park

Address: 3803 30th Avenue

Phone: 308-237-4644

Hours: Open 7:00 am to 10:00 pm.

L

LINCOLN

Oak Lake Dog Park

Address: 1st Street and Cornhuskers Highway

Richman's Run Dog Park

Address: 70th and Van Dorn

N

NORFOLK

TaHaZouka Dog Park

Address: South 13th Street

Hours: Open sunrise to sunset.

NORTH PLATTE

Waggin' Tails Dog Park

Address: West Leota Street

O

OMAHA

Hefflinger Dog Park

Address: Maple Street

Hours: Open sunrise to sunset.

S

SCOTTSBLUFF

Riverside Dog Park

Address: Beltline

Hours: Open daylight hours.

NORTH DAKOTA

B

BISMARK

Century Bark Park

Address: North 4th Street and East Century Avenue

Hours: Open 5:00 am to 11:00 pm.

BOWMAN

Bowman Dog Park

Address: 1 Street

F

FARGO

Yunker Farm Dog Park

Address: 12th Street and 28th Avenue North

Hours: Ope dawn to dusk.

Village West Dog Park

Address: 45th Street and 9th Avenue South

Hours: Open sunrise to sunset.

G

GRAND FORKS

Lincoln Dog Park

Address: Lincoln Drive

Phone: 701-746-2750

Hours: Open 5:00 am to 11:00 pm.

M

MINOT

Minot Dog Park

Address: 705 Highway 83 Bypass West

OKLAHOMA

D

DEL CITY

Wiggley Field Dog Park
Address: 140 Sunnylane

E

EDMOND

Edmond Dog Park
Address: Rankin and 33rd Street
Hours: Open sunrise to sunset.

M

MUSTANG

Mustang Dog Park
Address: 500 S.W 59th Street
Hours: Open 8:00 am to dusk.

N

NORMAN

Norman Community Dog Park

Address: 12th Avenue

Hours: Open sunrise to sunset.

O

OKLAHOMA CITY

OKC Paw Park and Dog Beach

Address: North Grand Boulevard and Hefner Parkway

Hours: Open sunrise to sunset.

T

TULSA

Biscuit Acres Bark Park

Address: 91st Street

Joe Station Bark Park

Address: 2279 Charles Page Boulevard

Hours: Open 5:00 am to 11:00 pm.

Y

YUKON

Pets and People Dog Park
Address: 701 Inla Avenue

SOUTH DAKOTA

S

SIOUX FALLS
Spencer Dog Park
Address: Cliff Avenue just south of I-229

Y

YANKTON
Marne Creek West Dog Park
Address: West City Limits Road and 23rd Street

TEXAS

A

ABILENE

Abilene KOA Dog Park
Address: 4851 West Stamford Street
FYI: Must be a camper to use the park.

ADDISON

Addison Dog Park
Address: Le Grande Avenue
Hours: Open 7:00 am to dusk.

Addison Dog Park
Address: Sidney Drive and Woodway Drive
Hours: Open 5:00 am to 11:00 pm.

ALLEN

Canine Commons Dog Park

Address: US 75 and Stacy Road

Phone: 972-678-4518

Hours: Open 7:00 am to 10:00 pm.

AMARILLO

John Stiff Memorial Dog Park

Address: Southwest 48th and Bell

Hours: Open 5:00 am to midnight.

Southeast Dog Park

Address: SE 46th and Osage

Hours: Open 5:00 am to midnight.

Thompson Dog Park

Address: NE 24th and Fillmore

Hours: Open 5:00 am to midnight.

ARLINGTON

Tails and Trails Dog Park

Address: 950 SE Green Oaks Boulevard

Hours: Open sunrise to sunset.

AUSTIN

West Austin Dog Park

Address: 1317 West 10th Street

Norwood Estates Dog Park

Address: 1009 Edgecliff Terrace

B

BAYTOWN

W.L. Jenkins Bark Park

Address: 4334 Crosby Cedar Bayou Road

BELLAIRE

Officer Lucy Dog Park

Address: 4337 Lafayette

Hours: Open 5:00 am to 9:30 pm.

C

COLLEGE STATION

Steeplechase Dog Park

Address: 301 Westridge Drive

Canine Station

Address: 300 Park Road

D

DALLAS

Bark Park Central

Address: Good Latimer Expressway and Commerce

Hours: Open 5:00 am to midnight. Closed Monday.

Central Dog Park
Address: 4711 Westside Drive
Hours: Open sunrise to sunset.

Downtown Dog Park
Address: Liberty near Swiss Avenue

Unleashed Indoor Dog Park
Address: Samuell Boulevard near Ferguson
Hours: Open 9:00 am to 9:00 pm Monday through Friday. 8:00 am to 9:00 pm Saturday and 10:00 am to 8:00 pm Sunday.
Fees: $7.50 daily or $150.00 monthly.

White Rock Lake Dog Park
Address: 8000 Mockingbird Lane
Hours: Open 5:00 am to midnight. Closed the 2nd and 4th Monday of each month.

DEER PARK
Ella and Friends Dog Park
Address: 500 West 13th Street

DENTON
Wiggly Field Dog Park
Address: 1400 Ryan Road
Hours: Closed Wednesday 7:00 am to 3:30 pm.

DISCOVERY GREEN
Discovery Green Dog Park
Address: 1500 McKinney
Phone: 713-400-7336

E
EL PASO
Eastwood Dog Park
Address: 3110 Parkwood Drive

EULESS

Villages of Bear Creek Dog Park

Address: 1951 Bear Creek Parkway

Phone: 817-685-1429

Hours: Open daylight hours. Closed Thursday.

F

FORT WORTH

Fort Woof Dog Park

Address: 450 Gateway Park

Hours: Open 5:00 am to 11:30 pm.

G

GEORGETOWN

Georgetown Bark Park

Address: 151 Holly Street

Hours: Open sunrise to sunset.

GRAND PRAIRIE

Central Bark Grand Prairie Dog Park
Address: 2222 West Warrior Trail
Hours: Open sunrise to sunset.

H

HOUSTON

Bill Archer Dog Park
Address: 3201 State Highway 6 North
Hours: Open 7:00 am to dusk.

Danny Jackson Bark Dog Park
Address: 4828 ½ Loop Central Drive
Hours: Open 7:00 am to dusk.

Ervan Chew Dog Park
Address: 4502 Dunlavy
Hours: Open 6:00 am to 11:00 pm.

Levy Dog Park
Address: 3801 Eastside
Hours: Open 6:00 am to 11:00 pm.

Maxey Park Bark and Run Dog Park
Address: 601 Maxey Road
Hours: Open 6:00 am to 11:00 pm.

Millie Bush Bark Dog Park
Address: 16756 Westheimer Parkway
Hours: Open 7:00 am to dusk.

San Felipe Dog Park
Address: 1717 Allen Parkway

Tanglewood Bark Park
Address: Bering and Woodway

TC Jester Dog Park
Address: TC Jester Boulevard

West Webster Dog Park
Address: 1501 West Webster Street

HUNTSVILLE
Pineview Dog Park
Address: 2335 23rd Street

K

KATY
Katy Dog Park
Address: 5414 Franz Road

KINGWOOD
AABY Dog Park
Address: 619 Lakeville Drive
Hours: Open sunrise to sunset.
FYI: Must register to use the park.

L

LAKEWAY

Lakeway City Dog Park

Address: 502 Hurst Creek Road

Hours: Open 6:00 am to 10:00 pm (Daylight Savings Time) and 6:00 am to 8:00 pm (Standard Time)

LEWISVILLE

Railroad Dog Park

Address: Railroad Street and Bennett Lane

M

MARSHALL

The Pet Place Dog Park

Address: 1901 Jefferson Avenue

Phone: 903-938-7297

Hours: Open 10:00 am to 5:00 pm. Closed Saturday, Sunday and Holidays.

MIDLAND

Hogan's Run Dog Park

Address: East Wadley Avenue

Hours: Open sunrise to sunset.

N

NORTH RICHLAND HILLS

Tipps Canine Hollow

Address: 7804 Davis Boulevard

Hours: Open 8:00 am to dusk.

O

OLMITO

Catherine Brown Stillman Dog Park

Address: 416 FM 511

P

PASADENA

Pasadena Animal Shelter Dog Park
Address: 5150 Burke Road
Phone: 281-991-0602

Bay Area Park Dog Park
Address: Bay Area Boulevard
Hours: Open 7:00 am to dusk.

PEARLAND

Southdown Dog Park
Address: 2150 County Road 94

Independence Dog Park
Address: 3919 Liberty Drive

PLANO

Jack Carter Dog Park

Address: 6500 Roundrock Trail

Hours: Open sunrise to sunset. Closed the first and third Tuesday of each month.

R

ROUND ROCK

Round Rock Dog Depot

Address: 800 Deerfoot Drive

Hours: Open 6:00 am to 8:00 pm April through October 1st and 6:00 am to 6:00 pm October 2nd through March.

S

SAN ANTONIO

McAllister Dog Park

Address: Starcrest Drive

Hours: Open 5:00 am to 11:00 pm.

Pearsall Dog Park
Address: 4700 Old Pearsall Road
Hours: Open 5:00 am to 11:00 pm.

SAN MARCOS
San Marcos Dog Park
Address: 625 East Hopkins

SOUTHLAKE
Boo Boo's Buddies Dog Park
Address: 3901 North White Chapel
Hours: Open sunrise to sunset.

SUGAR LAND
Sugar Land Palm Springs Dog Park
Address: Commonwealth and University Boulevards
Phone: 281-275-2885
Hours: Open sunrise to sunset.

W

WOODLANDS

Terramont Small Dog Park
Address: 8500 Terramont Drive
Hours: Open sunrise to sunset.

Cattail Dog Park
Address: 9323 Cochran's Crossing Drive
Hours: Open sunrise to sunset.

Bear Branch Dog Park
Address: 5200 Research Forest Drive
Hours: Open sunrise to sunset.

WISCONSIN

A

APPLETON

Outagamie County Pet Exercise Park

Address: French Road

Hours: Open 7:00 am to dusk. Closed in the winter.

C

CROSS PLAINS

Indian Lake Dog Park

Address: 8183 Highway 19

E

EAU CLAIRE

Eau Claire Dog Park

Address: 4503 House Road

Hours: Open sunrise to sunset.

F
FOND DU LAC
Lakeside Dog Park
Address: Lakeside Drive

G
GRAFTON
Muttland Meadows Dog Park
Address: 2020 South Green Bay Road

H
HOBART
Brown County Dog Park
Address: West Mason (Highway 54) at Hillcrest Road
Phone: 920-448-6242
Hours: Open 8:00 am to sunset
Fees: $15.00 annually or $2.00 day use pass at the park.

J

JANESVILLE

Paw Print Park

Address: Oakhill Avenue

K

KAUKANA

Kaukana Dog Park

Address: Farmland Drive

L

LA CROSSE

Myrick Dog Park

Address: 2000 La Crosse Street

M

MADISON

Warner Dog Park

Address: Sheridan Drive

Fees: Annual tag $23.00 or a daily fee of $4.00.

Sycamore Dog Park

Address: 4517 Sycamore Park

Fees: Annual tag $23.00 or a daily fee of $4.00.

Quann Dog Park

Address: 1802 Expo Drive

Hours: Open sunrise to sunset.

Fees: Annual tag $23.00 or a daily fee of $4.00.

MANITOWOC

Marina Retention Area Dog Park

Address: Maritime Drive

Phone: 920-683-4530

MIDDLETOWN

Middletown Dog Park

Address: Left side of County Highway Q.

Fees: Annual tag $23.00 or a daily fee of $4.00.

MILTON

Tails N Trails Dog Park

Address: Elm Street and West High Street

Hours: Open sunrise to sunset.

MILWAUKEE

Granville Dog Park

Address: West Goodhope Road

Hours: Open 7:00 am to dusk.

Estabrook Dog Park

Address: Wilson Drive and Estabrook Parkway

Hours: Open sunrise to sunset.

Fees: $20.00 annually.

N

NASHOTAH

Nashotah Dog Park

Address: West 330 North 5113 County Trunk Highway C

Phone: 262-548-7801

Hours: Open sunrise to 10:00 pm.

Fees: $3.00 parking fee on weekdays and $5.00 parking fee on weekends and holidays.

O

OAK CREEK

Runway Dog Park

Address: 1214 East Rawson Avenue

Hours: Open sunrise to sunset.

Fees: $20.00 annually or $5.00 day use pass.

OSH KOSH

Winnebago County Community Dog Park

Address: East Snell Road

Hours: Open 7:00 am to 11:00 pm.

P

PRAIRIE DU SAC

Shamrock Dog Park

Address: East 11340 County Road PF

Phone: 608-643-2451

Hours: Open 7:00 am to 6:00 pm Monday through Friday and 8:00 am to noon Saturday. Closed Sunday.

Fees: $85.00 annually or $2.00 day permit.

R
ROME
Room to Roam Dog Park
Address: Apache Avenue

S
STEVENS POINT
Standing Rocks Dog Park
Address: 7695 Standing Rock Road
Fees: $20.00 annual fee.

STOUGHTON
Viking Dog Park
Address: 2525 County Highway B

SUN PRAIRIE
Sun Prairie Dog Park
Address: South Bird
Hours: Open sunrise to sunset.

T

TOMAHAWK

Tomahawk Dog Park

Address: West Somo Avenue

Fees: $2.00 per visit

TWO RIVERS

Riverside Dog Park

Address: 1423 River Place

V

VERONA

Badger Prairie Dog Park

Address: 6720 Highway 151

VILLAGE OF WESTON

Weston Dog Park

Address: Meridian Avenue and Regent

Hours: Open 6:00 am to 11:00 pm.

W

WAUKESHA

Minooka Dog Park

Address: 1927 East Sunset Drive

Hours: Open sunrise to 10:00 pm.

Fees: Parking fee $3.00 on weekdays, $5.00 on weekends or $25.00 annually for residents and $36.00 for non residents.

WAUNAKEE

Ripp Dog Park

Address: Ripp Road and Dorn Drive

WAUPACA

Waupaca County Dog Park

Address: 601 Highway K

Phone: 715-258-6243

WESTPORT

Yahara Heights Dog Park

Address: 5428 State Highway 113 and Catfish Court

Fees: $23.00 annually or $4.00 daily fee.

ALABAMA

A

AUBURN

Kiesel Park

Address: 520 Chadwick Lane

Hours: Open sunrise to sunset.

B

BIRMINGHAM

George Ward Park

Address: Green Springs Highway

Hours: Open sunrise to sunset.

D

DAPHNE

Daphne Dog Park At Al Trione Sports Complex

Address: 8600 Whispering Pines Road

Phone: 251-621-3703

Hours: Open sunrise to sunset.

G

GULF SHORES

Gulf Shores Dog Park

Address: 260 Clubhouse Road

H

HUNTSVILLE

Dog Spot

Address: 100 Cleveland Street

Hours: Open sunrise to sunset.

M

MADISON

Dog Spot at Creekwood Park

Address: 360 Harvestwood Court

Hours: Open sunrise to sunset.

CONNECTICUT

B

BRANFORD

Branford Dog Park

Address: 421 Shore Drive

Young Pond Dog Park

Address: Route 146

E

ESSEX

Paw Park at Viney Hill

Address: Hillside Drive

Hours: Open sunrise to sunset.

G

GRANBY

Granby Doggs Park

Address: North Granby Road

GREENWICH

Grass Island Dog Park

Address: Shore Road

GROTON

Central Bark Dog Park at Copp Family Park

Address: Highway 184

H

HAMDEN

Hamden Dog Park

Address: Ridge Road and Waite Street

Hours: Open sunrise to sunset.

M

MIDDLEFIELD

Middlefield Dog Park

Address: Mattabesek Road

Hours: Open sunrise to sunset.

N

NEW CANAAN

Spencers Run Dog Park

Address: Lapham Road

Hours: Open sunrise to sunset.

NORWICH

Pawsitive Park

Address: 261 Asylum Street

R

RIDGEFIELD

Bark Park

Address: Prospect Ridge Road

S

SOUTH WINDSOR

South Windsor Bark Park

Address: Chief Ryan Way

Hours: Open sunrise to sunset.

SOUTHINGTON

Southington Dog Park

Address: Mill Street

STAMFORD

Stamford Dog Park

Address: East Main Street and Courtland Avenue

T

TRUMBULL

Trumbull Dog Park

Address: Indian Ledge Park Road and Whitney Avenue

W

WATERFORD

Stenger Farm Dog Park

Address: Clark Lane

WETHERSFIELD

Wethersfield Dog Park

Address: 154 Prospect Street

Hours: Open sunrise to sunset.

DELAWARE

M

MIDDLETOWN

Levels Road Dog Park

Address: Levels Road

Hours: Open 7:30 am to dusk.

N

NEWARK

Iron Hill Dog Park

Address: Old Baltimore Pike and Whitaker Road

W

WILMINGTON

Talley Day Bark Park

Address: 1300 Foulk Road

Phone: 302-571-4006

FLORIDA

A

APOPKA

Doctor's Dog Park

Address: 21 North Highland Avenue

Phone: 407-703-1741

Hours: Open 8:00 am to dusk.

B

BOCA RATON

Canine Cove at South County Regional Park

Address: 12551 Glades Road

Phone: 561-966-6664

Hours: Open sunrise to sunset. Closed Wednesdays, noon to 3:00 pm.

Mizner Dog Park
Address: 751 Banyan Trail
Phone: 561-393-7821
Hours: Open 7:30 am to dusk. Closed Wednesday until noon.

BRADENTON
Happy Tails Dog Park at G.T Bray Park
Address: 51st Street West and 29th Avenue West

C
CLEARWATER
Doggie Days Dog Park at Crest Lake Park
Address: 201 Glenwood Avenue
Hours: Open 6:00 am to 11:00 pm.

Sand Key Dog Park
Address: 1060 Gulf Boulevard

CORAL SPRINGS

Dr Paul's Pet Care Center Dog Park
Address: Sportsplex Drive
Hours: Open dawn to 9:30 pm.

D

DeLand
Barkley Square Dog Park
Address: 1010 North Ridgewood Avenue
Hours: Open sunrise to sunset.

DELRAY BEACH

Lake Ida Dog Park
Address: Lake Ida Road
Phone: 561-966-6664

DUNEDIN

Happy Tails Dog Park

Address: 3051 Garrison Road

Hours: Open 7:00 am to sunset.

E

ESTERO

K-9 Corral Dog Park at Estero Park

Address: 9200 Corkscrew Palms Boulevard

Phone: 239-533-7275

Hours: Open 7:00 am to 10:00 pm.

F

FORT LAUDERDALE

Bark Park at Snyder Park

Address: 3299 SW 4th Avenue

Hours: Open 7:00 am to 6:30 pm (November through March) and 7:00 am to 7:30 pm (April through October). Closed Christmas and New Years.

Fees: $1.00 per person on weekends. Free on weekdays.

River Walk Linear Dog Park
Address: 20 North New River Drive
Phone: 954-828-7275
Hours: Open 24 hours.

FORT MYERS

Barkingham Dog Park
Address: 9800 Buckingham Road
Phone: 239-533-7275
Hours: Open sunrise to sunset.

G

GAINESVILLE

Dog Wood Park

Address: 5505 SW Archer Road

Hours: Non-members 9:00 am to 5:00 pm (Saturday-Sunday), 1:00 pm – 4:00 pm (Tuesday, Wednesday, Thursday), 4:00 pm to 6:00 pm (Friday).

Hours for members are dawn to dusk. Closed Monday and Fridays to non-members.

Fees: Non-members, $9.00 for the first dog, $2.00 each additional dog. Membership $249 annually or $30.00 monthly.

H
HIALEAH
Amelia Earhart Bark Park
Address: 401 East 65th Street
Hours: Open sunrise to sunset.

HOLIDAY
Anclote Gulf Dog Park
Address: 2305 Bailies Bluff Road

HOLLYWOOD
Emerald Hills Lake Dog Park
Address: 3901 North 30th Terrace
Phone: 954-921-3404

John Williams Dog Park
Address: 6101 Sheridan Street
Phone: 954-921-3404

Oakridge Dog Park
Address: 5200 SW 35th Avenue
Phone: 954-921-3404

Poinciana Neighborhood Dog Park
Address: 1301 South 21st Avenue
Phone: 954-921-3404

HOMESTEAD
James Archer Smith Bark Park
Address: 300 NW 12th Street

Mayor Roscoe Warren Dog Park
Address: Palm Drive and SW 167th Avenue

I

INVERNESS

Bark Central Dog Park

Address: 6301 East Turner Camp Road

Phone: 352-341-2275

Hours: Open 8:00 am to 6:00 pm.

Fees: $300.00 annually or $30.00 monthly or $10.00 daily or $20.00 for two weeks.

ISLAMORADA

Founder's Park Dog Park

Address: 87032 Overseas Highway

Phone: 305-853-1685

J

JACKSONVILLE

Fresh Prints Forest Dog Park

Address: Beach Boulevard and Peach Drive

Phone: 904-642-9988

Hours: Members, sunrise to 8:30 pm. Non-members, 2:00 pm to 8:30 pm (Monday through Friday), 10:00 am to 8:30 pm (Saturday) and noon to 6:00 pm (Sunday).

Fees: $25.00 per month or $7.00 per visit.

Confederate Playground Dog Park

Address: 949 Hubbard Street

Phone: 904-630-2489

Hours: Open 8:00 am to 10:00 pm.

Dog Wood Park of Jacksonville
Address: 7407 Salisbury Road South
Fees: $11.00 one day pass, $289.00 annually, or $35.00 monthly.

Julington Creek Animal Walk
Address: 12075-300 San Jose Boulevard
Hours: 7:00 am to 7:00 pm (Monday-Friday), 8:00 am to 3:00 pm (Saturday), 4:00 pm to 6:00 pm (Sunday).
Fees: $12.00 day pass, $50.00 monthly or $275.00 annually.

JACKSONVILLE BEACH
Paws Park in Wingate Park
Address: 15 Street and Shetter
Hours: Open sunrise to sunset.

K

KEY WEST

Higgs Beach Dog Park

Address: White Street and Atlantic Boulevard

Hours: Open 6:00 am to 11:00 pm.

KISSIMMEE

Mill Slough Dog Park

Address: 2138 Agate Street

L

LAKELAND

Diogi Park at Loyce E. Harpe Park

Address: 500 West Carter Road

Phone: 863-499-2613

LAND O' LAKES

Land O'Lakes Recreation Complex Dog Park
Address: 3032 Collier Parkway

LUTZ

Carolyn Meeker Dog Park
Address: 122 1st Avenue SW
Hours: Sunrise to 7:00 pm.

M

MIAMI

Blanche Dog Park
Address: Shipping Avenue and Virginia Street

Lago Mar Dog Park
Address: SW 162nd Avenue and SW 80th Street
Hours: Open sunrise to sunset.

Martell Bark Park
Address: NE 36th Street

Northeast Regional Dog Park
Address: 16700 Biscayne Boulevard

The Dog Chow Dog Park
Address: 2600 South Bayshore Drive
Hours: Open sunrise to sunset.

Tropical Dog Park
Address: 7900 SW 40th Street
Phone: 305-226-8316
Hours: Open sunrise to sunset.

MIAMI BEACH
Belle Isle Dog Park
Address: Island Avenue on Belle Island
Phone: 305-861-3616

Flamingo Dog Park
Address: 1400 Michigan Avenue
Phone: 305-673-7766
Hours: Open 7:00 am to 9:00 pm.

Pinetree Dog Park
Address: 4400 Pinetree Drive
Phone: 305-673-7730
Hours: Open sunrise to sunset.

Washington Avenue Dog Park
Address: 201 South 2nd Street
Phone: 305-673-7766
Hours: Open sunrise to sunset.

MIAMI SPRINGS
Miami Springs Bark Park
Address: 751 Dove Avenue

N

NEW PORT RICHEY

Meadows Dog Park

Address: Larch Lane

NICEVILLE

Niceville Dog Park

Address: Highway 85 and College Boulevard

Hours: Open dawn to 8:00 pm.

NORTH FORT MEYERS

Pooch Dog Park

Address: 1297 Driftwood Drive

Phone: 239-533-7275

O

OAKLAND PARK

Bark Park
Address: 971 NW 38th Street
Phone: 954-630-4500
Hours: Open sunrise to sunset.

OLDSMAR

Mobbly Bayou Dog Park
Address: 423 Lafayette Boulevard

Sheffield Dog Park
Address: 1923 Cutty Bay Court

ORANGE PARK

Poochie's Swim and Play Park
Address: Oak Lane
Hours: Visitors, 3:00 pm to 6:00 pm (Wednesday – Friday), 10:00 am to 4:00 pm (Saturday-Sunday).
Fees: $10.00 per day or $30.00 per month.

ORLANDO

Barber Dog Park
Address: 3701 Gatlin Avenue

Barnett Dog Park
Address: 4801 West Colonial Drive

Downey Dog Park
Address: 10107 Flowers Avenue

Dr. Phillips Dog Park
Address: 8249 Buenavista Woods Boulevard

Meadow Woods Dog Park
Address: 1751 Rhode Island Woods Circle

P

PALM HARBOR

Chesnut Dog Park

Address: 2200 East Lake Road

PALMETTO BAY

Perrine Wayside Dog Park

Address: 16425 South Dixie Highway

Hours: Open sunrise to sunset.

Pembroke Pines

Pembroke Pines Bark Park

Address: 9751 Johnson Street

PENSACOLA

Ashton Brosnaham Dog Park

Address: 10370 Ashton Brosnaham Road

Hours: Open sunrise to sunset.

Bayview Dog Park and Beach
Address: 20th Avenue and Osceola Drive
Phone: 850-436-5511
Hours: Open 6:00 am to 9:00 pm.

Bill Dickinson Dog Park
Address: 3151 Fenceline Road
Phone: 850-475-5220
Hours: Open sunrise to sunset.

Lexington Terrace Dog Park
Address: 900 South Old Corry Field Road
Phone: 850-475-5220
Hours: Open sunrise to sunset.

Scott Complex Dog Park
Address: Summit Boulevard
Hours: Open 6:00 am to 9:00 pm.

PLANTATION

Happy Tails Dog Park

Address: 6600 SW 16th Street

Hours: Open 7:00 am to dusk.

PONCE INLET

Happy Tails Dog Park

Address: 4680 South Peninsula Drive

Hours: Open 6:00 am to 9:00 pm.

PONTE VEDRA

Paws Dog Park

2455 Palm Valley Road

Phone: 904-209-0370

Hours: Open 7:00 am to sunset.

S

SARASOTA

Lakeview Paw Park
Address: 7150 Lago Street
Hours: Open sunrise to sunset.

Paw Park North
Address: 4570 17th Street

SEBASTIAN

Keen Terrace Dog Park
Address: Wimbrow Drive

SEMINOLE

Boca Ciega Millenium Dog Park
Address: 12410 74th Avenue

ST. AUGUSTINE

Paws Dog Park

Address: 607 Old Beach Road

Paws Dog Park

Address: 1595 Wildwood Drive

Phone: 904-209-0385

Hours: Open sunrise to sunset.

ST. CLOUD

Partin Triangle Dog Park

Address: Neptune Road

Phone: 407-742-0100

ST. PETERSBURG

Coquina Key Dog Park
Address: 3595 Locust Street SE
Hours: Open sunrise to sunset.

Crescent Lake Dog Park
Address: 1320 5th Street North
Hours: Open sunrise to sunset.

Lake Vista Dog Park
Address: 1401 62nd Avenue South
Hours: Open sunrise to sunset.

North Shore Dog Park
Address: North Shore Drive and 7th Avenue
Hours: Open sunrise to sunset.

Walter Fuller Dog Park
Address: 7901 30th Avenue North
Hours: Open sunrise to sunset.

SUNNY ISLES BEACH

Bone Zone

Address: 17815 North Bay Road

Hours: Open 7:30 am to 8:30 pm.

SUNRISE

Barkham Dog Park

Address: 16001 West State Road 84

Phone: 954-389-2000

Hours: Open 8:00 am to 6:00 pm.

T

TAMARAC

Gary B. Jones Park for People and Pups

Address: 8101 Southgate Boulevard

TAMPA

Davis Islands Dog Beach
Address: 1002 Severn Street
Hours: Open sunrise to sunset.

Gadsden Dog Park
Address: 6901 South MacDill Avenue
Hours: Open sunrise to sunset.

Giddens Dog Park
Address: 5209 North 12th Street
Hours: Open sunrise to sunset.

James Urbanski Dog Park
Address: 4810 North Himes Avenue
Hours: Open sunrise to sunset.

Logan Gate Dog Park
Address: 7374 Monterey Boulevard

Palma Ceia Dog Park
Address: 2200 Marti Street
Hours: 8:00 am to sunset (Monday- Friday) and 9:00 am- sunset (Saturday – Sunday).

Rowlett Dog Park
Address: 2401 East Yukon
Hours: Open sunrise to sunset.

West Dog Park
Address: 6402 Occident Street
Hours: Open sunrise until 10:00 pm.

TARPON SPRINGS

Anderson Dog Park

Address: 39699 U.S Highway 19 North

TIERRA VERDE

Paw Playground

Address: 3500 Pinellas Bayway

Hours: Open 7:00 am to dark.

V

VENICE

Paw Park

Address: 1600 Harbor Drive South

Hours: Open sunrise to sunset.

Woodmere Paw Park South

Address: 3951 Woodmere Park Boulevard

Hours: Open sunrise to sunset.

W

WEST PALM BEACH

Pooch Pines

Address: 7715 Forest Hill Boulevard

Phone: 561-966-6664

Hours: Open sunrise to sunset. Closed Wednesdays noon to 3:00 pm.

WILTON MANORS

Colohatchee Bark Park

Address: 1975 NE 15th Avenue

Phone: 954-390-2130

Hours: 9:00 am to 6:00 pm (Monday, Thursday, Friday) and 9:00 am to noon (Saturday, Sunday).

Days closed: Tuesdays, Wednesdays and special events.

Fees: $30.00 for Wilton Manors residents and $60.00 for non-residents.

WINTER PARK

Fleet Peeples Off Leash Dog Area

Address: Lakemont Avenue

Hours: 8:00 am to sunset (Monday-Friday), 8:00-10:00 am and 4:00 pm to sunset (weekends and holidays).

Z

ZEPHYRHILLS

Meadowood Dog Park

Address: Meadowood Loop

GEORGIA

A

ACWORTH
Pitner Road Dog Park
Address: 2450 Pitner Road
Phone: 770-528-8890

ALPHARETTA
Waggy World Paw Park
Address: 175 Roswell Street
Phone: 678-297-6100
Hours: Open 8:00 am to sunset.

ATHENS
C.Spot Run Sandy Creek Dog Park
Address: Sandy Park Drive

Memorial Park Dog Park
Address: 293 Gran Ellen Drive

Wiggley Field
Address: Whit Davis Road

ATLANTA

Atlantic Station Dog Park
Address: State Street NW and 17th Street

Park Grounds
Address: 142 Flat Shoals Avenue SE
Phone: 678-528-9901
Hours: 7:00 am to 9:00 pm (Monday-Friday) and 8:00 am to 9:00 pm (Saturday-Sunday).

AUGUSTA

PKP Bark Park
Address: 1600 Troupe Street

B

BOGART

Pawtropolis Central Bark

Address: 130 Whitetail Way

Fees: $2.00 per visit.

C

CLARKSTON

Clarkston Dog Park

Address: Norman Road

Hours: Open sunrise to sunset.

CUMMING

Windermere Dog Park

Address: 3355 Windermere Parkway

D

DECATUR

Adair Dog Park
Address: Trinity Place

Glenlake Dog Park
Address: 1121 Church Street and Norris Street

Mason Mill Dog Park
Address: 1340 McConell Street

Oakhurst Dog Park
Address: 450 East Lake Drive

DUNWOODY

Henry Jones Dog Park
4770 North Peachtree Road
Hours: Open sunrise to sunset.

G

GAINESVILLE

Laurel Bark Park

Address: 3100 Old Cleveland Highway

Phone: 770 535-8280

H

HAMPTON

North Mt. Carmel

Address: 307 North Mt. Carmel Road

K

KENNESAW

Swift-Cantrell Dog Park

Address: Old 41 Highway NW

L

LAWRENCEVILLE

Ronald Reagan Dog Park

Address: 2777 Five Forks Trickum Road

M

MACON

Tyler's Place Dog Park
Address: Chestnut Street
Hours: Open sunrise to sunset.

MARIETTA

Lewis Dog Park
Address: 475 Campbell Street

Sweat Mountain Dog Park
Address: 4346 Steinhauer Road
Hours: Open sunrise to sunset.

MILTON

Wolfbrook Dog Park
Address: 13665 New Providence Road
Phone: 770-772-0440
Hours: Open sunrise to sunset.
Fees: $120.00 per quarter.

N

NEWTON

Newton Dog Park

Address: 3125 Old Alabama Road

NORCROSS

Graves Dog Park

Address: 1540 Graves Road

Phone: 770-339-3200

Pinckneyville Dog Park

Address: 4758 South Old Peachtree Road

Phone: 770-339-3200

P

PEACHTREE

Peachtree City Dog Park

Address: McIntosh Trail

Hours: Open sunrise to sunset.

R

ROSWELL

Leita Thompson Memorial Dog Park
Address: 1355 Woodstock Road

S

SAVANNAH

The Savannah Dog Park
Address: 41st and Drayton Street

SMYRNA

Burger Dog Park
Address: 680 Glendale Pace SE
Phone: 770-431-2842

Lake Court Dog Park
Address: Lake Court

SNELLVILLE

Lenora Dog Park

Address: 4515 Lenora Church Road

Phone: 770-339-3200

STONE MOUNTAIN

Red Dog Park

Address: 3rd and Pools Street

Hours: Open 6:00 am to 9:00 pm.

T

TYBEE ISLAND

Tybee Island Dog Park

Address: Van Horne and Fort Street

Hours: Open sunrise to sunset.

INDIANA

A

ANDERSON
Canine Companion Corral
Address: 2108 West 8th Street

AVON
Avon-Washington Township Paw Park
Address: County Road 575 East
Phone: 317-272-1835
Fees: $50.00 annually

B

BEECH GROVE
Paw Patch Dog Park
Address: 1300 Churchman Avenue
Hours: Open sunrise to sunset.
Fees: $35.00 annually + $10.00 key card fee.

BLOOMINGTON

Karst Farm Dog Park

Address: 5200 West Airport Road

Fees: $75.00 annually.

C

CARMEL

Club Canine Dog Park

Address: 457 3rd Avenue SW

Phone: 317-569-1191

Hours: Open the first and third Fridays of each month from 6:30 pm to 8:00 pm.

Fees: $5.00 for non-members for the evening.

CROWN POINT

Dogwood Run

Address: 6322 West 133rd Avenue

E

EVANSVILLE

Central Bark

Address: First Avenue

Hours: Open sunrise to sunset.

F

FISHERS

Pierson Bark Park

Address: 11787 East 131st

Hours: Open sunrise to sunset.

Fees: $139.00 annually, $30.00 monthly or $7.00 daily.

FORT WAYNE

Pawster Park Pooch Playground

Address: Winchester Road

Hours: Open 6:00 am to 10:00 pm.

FRANKLIN

Province Dog Park
Address: Province Park
Hours: Open sunrise to sunset.
Fees: $30.00 annually for residents and $45.00 annually for non-residents.

G

GOSHEN

Robert L. Nelson Dog Park
Address: 60376 CR 13
Hours: Open sunrise to sunset.
Fees: Members only.

GREENWOOD

Four Paws Dog Park
Address: 200 Legacy Boulevard
Phone: 317-881-4545
Hours: Open sunrise to sunset.
Fees: $40.00 (non-residents) and $30.00 (residents).

H

HIGHLAND

Wicker Memorial Dog Park

Address: Ridge Road

I

INDIANAPOLIS

Broad Ripple Dog Park

Address: 1550 Broad Ripple Avenue

Fees: $50.00 annually + $10.00 gate key.

Gilmer Canine Companion Zone

Address: 7840 West 56th Street

Fees: $50.00 annually + $10.00 gate key.

Humane Society of Indianapolis Dog Park

Address: 7929 Michigan Road

Phone: 317-872-5650

Hours: 9:00 am to 7:00 pm (Fall-Winter) and 7:00 am to 9:00 pm (Spring-Summer)

Fees: $50.00 annually + $10.00 gate key.

Paul Ruster Dog Park

Address: 11300 East Prospect Street

Hours: Open sunrise to sunset.

Fees: $50.00 annually + $10.00 gate key.

K

KOKOMO

Kokomo Dog Park

Address: Carter Street

Hours: Open sunrise to sunset.

L

LAFAYETTE

Shamrock Dog Park

Address: Wabash Avenue

Hours: Open sunrise to sunset.

Fees: $60.00 annually or $5.00 day permit.

LAWRENCE

Waggin Tails Bark Park
Address: 10450 East 63rd Street
Phone: 317-549-4815
Fees: $30.00 (resident) and $40.00 (non-resident) plus a one time $25.00 key deposit.

LOWELL

Freedom Bark Park
Address: 17105 Cline Avenue

M

MADISON

Madison Dog Park
Address: Vaughn Drive
Fees: $12.00 annually.

MICHIGAN CITY

Bark Park

Address: 7943 West 400 North

Phone: 219-325-8315

Fees: $2.00 (resident) or $3.00 (non-resident) day use or $20.00 (resident), $25.00 (non-resident) annually.

MUNSTER

Centennial Dog Park

Address: 9701 Calumet Avenue

Phone: 219-836-7275

Fees: $50.00 annually (resident) or $175.00 annually (non-resident).

R

RICHMOND

Hill's Bark Park

Address: Sylvan Nook Drive

V

VALPARAISO

Canine Country Club
Address: 3556 Sturdy Road
Hours: Open 7:00 am to dusk.
Fees: Membership ($120.00 annually) or a day permit $5.00.

Coco's Canine Cabana Indoor Dog Park
Address: 405 Elm Street
Phone: 219-462-1222
Hours: 5:00 am to 10:00 pm (Monday through Friday) and 8:00 am to 8:00 pm (Saturday and Sunday).
Fees: $2.50 per visit, per dog.

W

WESTFIELD

Bed & Biscuit Dog Park
Address: 3809 State Road 32 Westminster
Phone: 317-867-2663

WESTVILLE

Bark Park

Address: 3855 South 1100 Westminster

Phone: 219-325-8315

Fees: $2.00 (resident) or $3.00 (non-resident) for day use or $20.00 (resident), $25.00 (non-resident) annually.

KENTUCKY

A

ASHLAND

Ashland Boyd County Dog Park

Address: West Summit Road and US 60

B

BOWLING GREEN

Hills Bark Park

Address: Debbie Drive and Shawnee Way

BURLINGTON

Boone County Dog Park

Address: 5550 Idlewild Road

C

COVINGTON

Kenton Paw Dog Park

Address: 3950 Madison Pike

Hours: Open sunrise to sunset.

F

FORT THOMAS

Fort Thomas Dog Park

Address: Mayfield

Hours: Open sunrise to sunset.

FRANKFORT

East Frankfort Bark Park

Address: Myrtle Street

Hours: Open 8:00 am to dark.

L

LEXINGTON

Coldstream Dog Park
Address: McGrathiana Parkway

Jacobson Dog Park
Address: Richmond Road
Hours: Open sunrise to sunset.

Materson Station Dog Park
Address: Ruffian Way

Wellington Dog Park
Address: 565 Wellington Way

LOUISVILLE

Cochran Hill Dog Park

Address: 745 Cochran Hill Road

Fees: $15.00 for the first dog and $5.00 per additional dog in the same household.

Sawyer Dog Park

Address: 3000 Freys Hill Road

Fees: $25.00 for the first dog and $15.00 for the second dog and $5.00 per additional dog in the same household.

Vettiner Dog Run

Address: 5550 Charlie Vettiner Park Road

Fees: $15.00 for the first dog and $10.00 for the second dog and $5.00 per additional dog in the same household.

M

MURRAY

Murray-Calloway County Dog Park

Address: Arcadia Circle

P

PARIS

Patrick Brannon Dog Park

Address: Ford Mill Road

R

RICHMOND

Judy Rains Memorial Dog Park

Address: Lake Reba Drive

V

VERSAILLES

Dog Park at County Park

Address: Beasley Road and U.S 62 West

MAINE

B

BELFAST

Belfast Dog Park

Address: Route 52

P

PORTLAND

Valley Street Dog Park

Address: Valley Street

Ocean Avenue Dog Park

Address: Ocean Avenue

Quarry Run Dog Park

Address: Ocean and Portland

W

WEST KENNEBUNK

Kennebunk Dog Park

Address: 36 Sea Road

Hours: Open sunrise to sunset.

MARYLAND

A

ANDREWS AIR FORCE BASE
Liberty Dog Park
Address: Tuskegee Drive

ANNAPOLIS
Quiet Water Dog Park
Address: 600 Quiet Waters Park Road
Hours: Open sunrise to sunset.

ARNOLD
Broadneck Dog Park
Address: College Parkway and Broadneck Road
Hours: Open sunrise to sunset.

B

BALTIMORE

Canton Dog Park
Address: South Bouldin and Toone Street

Locust Point Dog Park
Address: East Fort Avenue
Fees: $20.00 annually.

BEL AIR

The Ma and Pa Dog Park
Address: 703 North Tollgate Road
Phone: 410-638-3305

BETHESDA

Cabin John Regional Dog Park
Address: 10900 Westlake Drive
Hours: Open sunrise to sunset. Closed Tuesdays 9:00 am to 11:00 am.

BOWIE
Bowie Dog Park
Address: 3600 Northview Drive

BOYDS
Black Hill Regional Dog Park
Address: 20030 Ridge Drive

C
COLLEGE PARK
College Park Dog Park
Address: Metzerott
Hours: Open sunrise to sunset.
Fees: $30.00

E

ELLICOT CITY

Worthington Dog Park

Address: 8170 Hillsborough Road

Phone: 410-313-4455

Hours: Open 7:00 am to dusk.

Fees: Daily permit $5.00 or $40.00 annually.

F

FALLSTON

Rebel's Dog Park

Address: 2208 Connolly Road

Phone: 410-836-1090

Hours: Open 7:00 am until shelter close.

G

GAITHERSBURG

Gaithersburg Dog Park

Address: 151 Bickerstaff Way

Phone: 301-258-6343

Fees: Guest pass $50.00

GAMBRILLS

Bell Branch Dog Park

Address: 2400 Davidsonville Road

Hours: Open sunrise to sunset.

GERMANTOWN

Ridge Road Recreational Dog Park

Address: 21155 Frederick Road

GREENBELT

Greenbelt Dog Park

Address: Hanover Drive

Phone: 301-345-5417

H

HYATTSVILLE

Heurich Dog Park

Address: Ager Road and Nicholson Street

Phone: 301-985-5020

L

LA PLATA

Turkey Hill Dog Park

Address: 9430 Turkey Hill Road

Hours: Open 8:00 am to dusk. Closed Christmas and New Years.

LAUREL

Dog Playground

Address: Van Dusen Road and Alan Drive

Maryland City Dog Park

Address: 565 Brock Bridge Road

LEXINGTON PARK

John G. Lancaster Dog Park

Address: 21550 Willows Road

Phone: 301-475-4200 ext 1800

Hours: Open sunrise to sunset.

O

OCEAN CITY

Ocean City Dog Playground

Address: 94th Street

Hours: Open sunrise to sunset.

Fees: $50.00 residents, $100 non-residents or a $15.00 one week pass.

P

PRINCE FREDERICK

Prince Frederick Dog Park

Address: 2695 Grays Road

Hours: Open sunrise to sunset.

R

REISTERSTOWN

BARC Park

Address: 12035 Reisterstown Road

Phone: 410-887-1142

Fees: $25.00 annually.

ROCKVILLE

King Farm Dog Park

Address: Pleasant Drive

Phone: 240-314-8700

S

SILVER SPRING

Wheaton Regional Dog Park

Address: Orebaugh Avenue

U

URBANA

Greenbriar Dog Park

Address: 3051 Thurston Road

Hours: Open sunrise to sunset.

W

WHITE PLAINS

White Plains Dog Park

Address: End of Demarr Road

Hours: Open 8:00 am to dusk. Closed Christmas and New Years.

MASSACHUSETTS

B

BOSTON

Carleton Court Dog Park
Address: Carlton and Holyoke Street

Charlesgate Dog Run
Address: Massachusetts Avenue and Beacon Street

Joe Wex Dog Park
Address: Washington Street
Hours: Open 6:00 am to 10:00 pm.

BROOKLINE

Brookline Avenue Playground Dog Park
Address: 575 Brookline Avenue
Hours: Open dawn to 1:00 pm (April – November), dawn to dusk (December through March).

C

CAMBRIDGE

Danehy Dog Park

Address: New Street and Danehy Park

Fort Washington Dog Park

Address: Waverly Street

Hours: Open sunrise to sunset.

Fresh Pond Reservation Dog park

Address: 250 Fresh Pond Way

Hours: Open sunrise to sunset.

Pacific Street Dog Park

Address: Tudor Street

Hours: Open sunrise to sunset.

D
DENNIS ON CAPE COD
Fresh Pond Dog Park
Address: Route 134

E
EGREMONT
French Park Dog Park
Address: 21 Prospect Lake Road

L
LOWELL
Lowell Dog Park
Address: First Street

M

MEDWAY

Henry Garnsey Canine Recreation Park

Address: Cottage Street

Hours: Open 6:30 am to dusk weekdays and 8:00 am to dusk weekends.

P

PROVINCETOWN

Pilgrim Bark Park

Address: Route 6 and Shank Painter Road

Hours: Open sunrise to sunset.

S

SALEM

Lelie's Retreat Dog Park

Address: Routes 114 near Route 107

Fees: $25.00 annually.

SHARON

Sharon Dog Park

Address: East Foxboro Street

SOMERVILLE

Ed Leathers Community Dog Park

Address: Skilton Avenue

Nunziato Field Dog Park

Address: Summer Street and Vianl Avenue

SOUTH BOSTON

South Boston Dog Park

Address: Columbia Road and William J. Day Boulevard

Hours: Open 6:00 am to 8:00 pm.

MICHIGAN

A

ADA

Shaggy Pines Dog Park

Address: 3895 Cherry Lane Avenue SE

Hours: Open 7:00 am to 9:00 pm.

Fees: $326.00 annually or $256.00 weekends only or $37.00 for one month or $10.00 day use. (there is an extra initial fee of $39.00).

ANN ARBOR

Olson Dog Park

Address: Dhu Varren Road

Fees: $50.00 annual Ann Arbor City off leash dog permit. $25.00 for extra dogs.

Swift Run Dog Park
Address: Ellsworth Road
Hours: Open sunrise to sunset. Closed Monday 8:30 am to 11:30 am and Friday 12:30 pm to 3:00 pm.
Fees: $50.00 annual Ann Arbor City off leash dog permit. $25.00 for extra dogs.

B
BAY CITY
Bay County Dog Park
Address: 800 Livingston Street

C
CLINTON TOWNSHIP
Clinton Township Dog Park
Address: 40700 Romeo Plank Road
Phone: 586-286-9336

D

DETROIT

Balduck Dog Park

Address: Chandler Park Drive

Hours: Open sunrise to sunset.

F

FLUSHING

Woof Woods Dog Park

Address: 7185 Gilette Road

Phone: 810-659-5951

Hours: Open 9:00 am to dusk.

Fees: $35.00 first year, $15.00 annually thereafter.

FRANKENMUTH

Hund Platz

Address: East Tuscola Road

G

GARDEN CITY

Me & My Shadow Swim and Fitness Center For Dogs
Address: 29855 Ford Road, Suite C
Phone: 734-525-9500
Hours: Open 10:00 am to 1:00 pm and 2:30 pm to 8:00 pm Tuesday through Saturday. Closed Sunday and Monday.

GRAND RAPIDS

Pet Supplies Plus Dog Park
Address: Lyon and Benjamin NE
Hours: Open sunrise to sunset.

GROSS POINTE SHORES

Gross Pointe Shores Dog Park
Address: Vernier and Lake Shore Drive

GROSS POINTE WOODS

Grosse Point Woods Dog Park
Address: Lakeshore Drive
Phone: 313-343-2470
Fees: Residents only. $20.00

H

HOLLAND

Ottawa County Dog Park
Address: 1286 Ottawa Beach Road

HOWELL

EZ Dog Park and Training
Address: 230 Norlynn Drive
Phone: 810-599-6669
Hours: Open 24 hours.
Fees: $40.00 per month.

J

JACKSON

New Paw Playground

Address: 1515 Carmen Drive

Hours: Open sunrise to sunset.

L

LAKE ORION

Orion Oaks Dog Park

Address: 2301 West Clarkston Road

Hours: Open sunrise to sunset.

Fees: Parking fees, $7.00 (resident) or $12.00 (non-resident) or annually $30.00 (resident) or $46.00 (non-resident).

LANSING

Soldan Dog Park

Address: 1601 East Cavanaugh Road

Hours: Open sunrise to sunset.

LOWELL

Lowell Dog Park

Address: Bowes Road

Phone: 616-897-6677

Hours: Open daylight hours.

M

MANISTEE

Manistee Dog Park

Address: First Street

MOUNT CLEMENS

Behnke Memorial Dog Park

Address: 300 North Groesbeck Highway

MUSKEGON

Dog Star Ranch

Address: 4200 Whitehall Road

Fees: $10.00 day rate or up to $256-$356 annually depending on the use package.

Kruse Dog Beach Off Leash Area
Address: West Sherman Boulevard

N

NORTHVILLE

Cady Street Dog Park
Address: 215 West Cady Street
Fees: $25.00- $50.00 annually (one time $25.00 gate key).

Community Dog Park
Address: Beck Road
Fees: $25.00- $50.00 annually (one time $25.00 gate key).

P

PLEASANT RIDGE

Pleasant Ridge Dog Run

Address: Ridge Road

Phone: 248-541-2900

Fees: $25.00 for residents or $60.00 for non-residents.

R

ROYAL OAK

Mark Twain Dog Park

Address: Campbell Road

Fees: $40.00 residents or $65.00 non-residents ($10.00 one time gate key).

S

SAGINAW

Steven A. Kirshenbaum Memorial Bark Park

Address: Midland Road

Hours: Open 8:00 am to dusk.

Fees: $2.00 parking fee or $0.50 walk-in.

SAUGATUCK

Tails and Trails Dog Park

Address: 134th Avenue

ST CLAIR SHORES

Statler Maloof Bark Park

Address: 19800 Chalon Street

Fees: $20.00 resident and $30.00 non-resident.

ST JOSEPH

Kiwanis Dog Park

Address: Pearl Street

Phone: 269-983-6341

W

WARREN

Anne Fracassa Memorial Dog Park

Address: Pauline Street and 12 Mile Road

Hours: Open 7:00 am to dusk.

Fees: $10.00 resident and $20.00 non-resident.

WEBSTER TOWNSHIP

Paw Run Recreation Area

Address: North Territorial Road

Fees: $220.00 annually or $4.00 per day.

WEST BLOOMFIELD

Karner Farm Dog Park

Address: 5911 Halsted Road

Phone: 248-451-1901 ext 220

Fees: $20.00 residents only access.

WESTLAND

Hines Dog Park
Address: Merriman Road
Phone: 866-664-4637

WIXOM

Lyon Oaks Dog Park
Address: 52221 Pontiac Trail
Phone: 248-437-7345
Hours: Open sunrise to sunset.
Fees: Parking fees-$7.00 (resident) or $12.00 (non-resident) or $30.00 annually (resident), $46.00 annually (non-resident).

WYOMING

Wyoming Dog Park
Address: 1414 Nagel SW
Phone: 616-530-3164
Fees: $12.00 annually (resident), $24.00 annually (non-resident).

NEW HAMPSHIRE

A

AMHERST

American K9 Country's Dog Park
Address: 336 Route 101 at Camp Road
Phone: 603-672-8448
Hours: Open sunrise to sunset.

C

CONCORD

Concord Dog Park
Address: Old Turnpike Road and Manchester Street
Hours: Open sunrise to sunset.

D

DERRY

Derry Dog Park
Address: Fordway off Route 102
Hours: Open sunrise to sunset.

P

PORTSMOUTH

Portsmouth Dog Park

Address: Junkins Avenue

Hours: Open sunrise to sunset.

R

RAYMOND

Riverside Bark Dog Park

Address: Sundeen Parkway

ROCHESTER

Rochester Dog Park

Address: Taylor Avenue

Fees: $20.00 annually.

NEW JERSEY

B

BERKELEY

Robert J. Miller Air Dog Park
Address: Mule Road and Pinwald Keswick Road
Hours: Open 8:00 am to 4:00 pm.
Fees: $25.00 annually for the first dog and $10.00 for the second dog.

BLOOMFIELD

Brookdale Dog Park
Address: 1294 Broad South
Hours: 8:00 am to 6:00 pm (November – March) and 8:00 am to 8:00 pm (April -October).

Watsessing Dog Park
Address: Locust Avenue and Prospect Street
Hours: Open sunrise to sunset.

C

CHERRY HILL

Cooper River Dog Park

Address: North Park Drive

F

FRANKLIN TOWNSHIP

Colonial Dog Park

Address: Mettlers Road and Colonial Drive

Phone: 732-873-2459

H

HAMILTON

Veterans Memorial Dog Park

Address: Kuser Road

L

LAKEWOOD

Ocean County Dog Park

Address: 700 Route 88

Phone: 732-506-9090

Hours: Open 8:00 am to 4:00 pm.

Fees: $25.00 annually for the first dog and $10.00 for the second dog.

LINCROFT

Thompson Dog Park

Address: Newman Springs Road

Phone: 732-842-4000 ext 4256

Hours: 8:00 am to sunset.

LONG VALLEY

Long Valley Dog Park
Address: Route 517
Phone: 908-876-3232
Hours: Open 8:00 am to sunset.
Fees: $10.00 annually for residents and $15.00 for non-residents.

M

MARLBORO

Marlboro Dog Park
Address: Wyncrest Road
Phone: 732-536-0200

MORRISTOWN

Lewis Morris Dog Park
Address: 270 Mendham Road
Phone: 973-326-7654
Hours: Open 9:00 am to sunset.

MOUNT LAUREL

Laurel Acres Dog Run

Address: 1045 South Church Street

MOUNT OLIVE

Turkey Brook Dog Park

Address: Flanders Road

MOUNTAINSIDE

Echo Lake Dog Park

Address: Park Drive

Phone: 908-527-4900

O

OCEAN CITY

Cape May County Dog Park

Address: 45th Street and Haven Avenue

Hours: Open 8:00 am to sunset.

Fees: Paw Pass- $25.00 for residents, $35.00 non-residents or $10.00 for one week visitor pass.

OCEANPORT

Wolf Hill Recreation Area Dog Park

Address: Eatontown Boulevard

Phone: 732-229-7025

P

PINEBROOK

Montville Township Dog Park

Address: Changebridge Road

Fees: $15.00 annually for residents, $20.00 annually for non-residents.

PRINCETON

Rocky Top Dog Park

Address: 4106 State Highway 27

R

RANDOLPH

Randolph Township Dog Park

Address: 502 Millbrook Avenue

Phone: 973-989-7050

Hours: Open sunrise to sunset.

ROXBURY

Roxbury Dog Park

Address: Emmans Road

Fees: $20.00 annually

V

VOORHEES

Connolly Dog Park

Address: Main Street and Centennial Boulevard

Hours: Open sunrise to sunset.

W

WANTAGE

Wantage Dog Park
Address: 128 Route 628
Phone: 973-875-4141

NEW YORK

A
ALBANY

Department Of General Services Dog Park
Address: Erie Boulevard
Phone: 518-434-2489
Hours: Open sunrise to sunset.

Hartman Road Dog Park
Address: New Scotland Avenue and Hartland Road
Phone: 518-434-2489

Normanskill Farm Dog Park
Address: Delaware Avenue
Phone: 518-434-2489

Westland Hills Dog Park
Address: Colvin Avenue
Phone: 518-434-2489
Hours: Open sunrise to sunset.

B

BETHLEHEM

Methlehem Dog Park

Address: Delmar Bypass

Hours: Open 8:00 am to dusk.

Fees: $30.00 annually

BUFFALO

The Barkyard

Address: Porter Avenue

Hours: Open sunrise to sunset.

C

CARMEL

Sycamore Dog Park

Address: Long Pond Road

CORTLANDT MANOR

Sprout Brook Dog Park

Address: 130 Sprout Brook Road

Hours: Open sunrise to sunset.

E

ELMSFORD

Elmsford Dog Park

Address: North Evarts and Winthrop Avenue

F

FISHKILL

Doug Phillips Dog Park

Address: Route 52 and Doug Phillips Road

Phone: 845-896-0661

H

HUNTINGTON

West Hills County Park Dog Run

Address: Sweet Hollow Road

Phone: 631-854-4423

I

ITHACA

Ithaca Dog Park

Address: The head of Cayuga Lake

K

KATONAH

Canine Commons

Address: 135 Beaver Dam Road

Phone: 914-666-4534

Hours: Open 7:00 am to sunset.

Fees: $10.00 annually (residents) or $5.00 day pass.

L

LIVERPOOL

Wegmans Good Dog Park

Address: 2500 Cold Springs Road

Hours: Open sunrise to sunset.

M

MONROE

Smith's Clove Dog Park

Address: 133 Spring Street

Phone: 845-783-4906

Hours: Open 7:00 am to 11:00 pm.

MONTGOMERY

Thomas Bull Memorial Dog Park

Address: State Route 416

Phone: 845-457-4900

MOUNT KISCO

Mount Kisco Dog Park

Address: 295 North Bedford Road

N

NEW HARTFORD

New Hartford Dog Park

Address: Sherrill Brook Town Park

Fees: $35.00 annually (residents) and $70.00 annually (non-residents).

NEW ROCHELLE

Paws Place

Address: Broadfield Road

Phone: 914-654-2087

Hours: Open sunrise to sunset.

Fees: $50.00 annually (residents) and $100.00 annually (non-residents).

NEW YORK

Brooklyn Bridge Dog Park
Address: Adams Street

Carl Schurz Dog Park
Address: East End Avenue
Hours: Open 9:00 am to 9:00 pm.

Chelsea Waterside Dog Park
Address: 11th Avenue and 22nd Street

Coleman Square Dog Park
Address: Pike and Monroe
Hours: Open 9:00 am to 9:00 pm.

Cooper Dog Park
Address: Olive Street and Maspeth Avenue
Hours: Open 9:00 am to 9:00 pm.

Dewitt Clinton Dog Park
Address: West 52nd and West 54th
Hours: Open 9:00 am to 9:00 pm.

DiMattina Dog Park
Address: Woodhull Road
Hours: Open 9:00 am to 9:00 pm.

Dyker Beach Dog Park
Address: 7th Avenue and 86th Street
Hours: Open 9:00 am to 9:00 pm.

East River Dance Oval Dog Park
Address: East River at East 60th Street
Hours: Open 9:00 am to 9:00 pm.

Ewen Dog Park
Address: Riverdale to Johnson Avenue
Hours: Open 9:00 am to 9:00 pm.

Fish Bridge Dog Park
Address: Dover Street
Hours: Open 9:00 am to 9:00 pm.

Fort Tryon Park
Address: Margaret Corbin Drive
Hours: Open 9:00 am to 9:00 pm.

Frank S. Hackett Dog Park
Address: Riverdale Drive
Hours: Open 9:00 am to 9:00 pm.

Greenwich Village Dog Park
Address: Leroy Street

Highbridge Dog Park
Address: Amsterdam and Fort George Avenue
Hours: Open 9:00 am to 9:00 pm.

Hillside Dog Park
Address: Columbia Heights and Vine Street
Hours: Open 9:00 am to 9:00 pm.

Inwood Hill Dog Park
Address: West 207th and Seaman Avenue
Hours: Open 9:00 am to 9:00 pm.

J.Hood Wright Dog Park
Address: Fort Washington and Haven Avenue
Hours: Open 9:00 am to 9:00 pm.

Madison Square Dog Park
Address: Madison Avenue to 5th Avenue
Hours: Open 9:00 am to 9:00 pm.

Manhattan Beach Dog Park
Address: East of Ocean Avenue
Hours: Open 9:00 am to 9:00 pm.

Marcus Garvey Dog Park
Address: Madison Avenue and East 120th Street

McCarren Dog Park
Address: North 12th Street
Hours: Open 9:00 am to 9:00 pm.

McGolrick Dog Park
Address: North Henry Street and Driggs Avenue
Hours: Open 9:00 am to 9:00 pm.

Morningside Dog Park
Address: Morningside Avenue
Hours: Open 9:00 am to 9:00 pm.

North Chelsea Dog Park
Address: Pier 84 at West 44th Street

North End Avenue Islands Dog Park
Address: North End Avenue

Owls Head Dog Park
Address: 68th Street and Shore Road
Hours: Open 9:00 am to 9:00 pm.

Palmetto Playground Dog Park
Address: Atlantic Avenue
Hours: Open 9:00 am to 9:00 pm.

Pelham Bay Dog Park
Address: Middletown Road
Hours: Open 9:00 am to 9:00 pm.

Peter Detmold Dog Park
Address: West of FDR Drive
Hours: Open 9:00 am to 9:00 pm.

Riverside Dog Park 1
Address: Riverside Drive at West 72nd
Hours: Open 9:00 am to 9:00 pm.

Riverside Dog Park 2
Address: Riverside Drive at West 87th
Hours: Open 9:00 am to 9:00 pm.

Riverside Dog Park 3
Address: Riverside Drive at West 105th
Hours: Open 9:00 am to 9:00 pm.

Robert Moses Dog Park
Address: 41st and 42nd Streets
Hours: Open 9:00 am to 9:00 pm.

Seton Dog Park
Address: West 232nd Street and Independence Avenue
Hours: Open 9:00 am to 9:00 pm.

Sirius Dog Run
Address: Liberty Street at the Esplanade

St. Nicholas Dog Park
Address: St. Nicholas Avenue
Hours: Open 9:00 am to 9:00 pm.

Theodore Roosevelt Dog Park
Address: Central Park west at 81st Street
Hours: Open 9:00 am to 9:00 pm.

Thomas Jefferson Dog Park
Address: East 112th Street and FDR Drive
Hours: Open 9:00 am to 9:00 pm.

Tompkins Square Dog Park
Address: 1st Avenue to Avenue B
Hours: Open 9:00 am to 9:00 pm.

Union Square Dog Park
Address: 15th Street and Union Square West
Hours: Open 9:00 am to 9:00 pm.

Van Cortlandt Dog Park
Address: West 251st Street and Broadway
Hours: Open 9:00 am to 9:00 pm.

Washington Square Dog Park
Address: 5th Avenue and Waverly Place
Hours: Open 9:00 am to 9:00 pm.

Williamsbridge Oval Dog Park
Address: 3225 Reservoir Oval East
Hours: Open 9:00 am to 9:00 pm.

O

OSSINING

Cesar Lane Dog Park

Address: 235 Cedar Lane

Hours: Open sunrise to sunset.

Fees: $20.00 annually.

P

PEEKSKILL

Peekskill Dog Park

Address: 1795 Main Street

Phone: 914-734-7275

POUGHKEEPSIE

See Spot Run Off Leash Area

Address: Overlook Road off 55

Hours: Open sunrise to sunset.

S

SLEEPY HOLLOW

Kingsland Point Dog Park

Address: End of Palmer Avenue in Philipse Manor

Hours: Open 7:00 am to sunset.

Fees: $25.00 annually.

SMITHTOWN

Blydeburgh County Dog Park

Address: Veterans Memorial Highway

Phone: 631-854-3713

W

WHITE PLAINS

Bark Park at Baldwin Farm

Address: Main Street

Hours: Open sunrise to sunset.

NORTH CAROLINA

A

ASHEVILLE

Asheville Dog Park
Address: Amboy Road and Lyman Avenue
Phone: 828-350-0333

Azalea Dog Park
Address: Azalea Road

B

BOONE

Watauga Dog Park
Address: Don Hayes Road
Hours: Open 6:00 am to sunset.
Fees: $50.00 annually or $3.00 for a day pass.

BURLINGTON

Jiggs Askew Memorial Bark Park
Address: 1333 Overbrook Road
Phone: 336-222-5030
Hours: Open sunrise to sunset.

C
CARBORO

Anderson Community Park
Address: Highway 54 West

CHAPEL HILL

Chapel Hill's Southern Park
Address: Dogwood Drive

The Chapel Hill Dog Park
Address: Northern Park Drive

CHARLOTTE

Barkingham Park
Address: 2900 Rocky River Road
Hours: Open 7:30 am to sunset.

Davie Dog Park
Address: 4635 Pineville Matthews Road
Hours: Open 7:30 am to sunset.

Frazier Neighborhood Dog Park
Address: 1200 West 4th Street
Hours: Open 7:30 am to sunset.

Ray's Fetching Meadow
Address: 8711 Monroe Road
Hours: Open 7:30 am to sunset.

CONOVER

Riverbend Dog Park

Address: 6700 North NC 16 Highway

Fees: $20.00 annually

CORNELIUS

Swaney Pointe K-9 Park

Address: 18441 Nantz Road

Hours: Open 7:30 am to sunset.

D

DAVIDSON

The Preserve Dog Park

Address: 330 O'Henry Avenue

DURHAM

Durham Dog Park

Address: 5999 Woodlake Drive

Fees: Dogapalooza Tag- $12.00 annually (residents) or $20.00 annually (non-residents).

Northgate Dog Park

Address: 400 West Lavender Avenue

Fees: Dogapalooza Tag- $12.00 annually (residents) or $20.00 annually (non-residents).

E

ELON

K-9 Corner Dog Park

Address: 434 Cook Road

Phone: 336-449-9255

Hours: Open sunrise to sunset.

Fees: $20.00 annually.

EMPIE

Wilmington Dog Park

Address: Park Avenue and Independence

Hours: Open sunrise to sunset.

G

GASTONIA

George Poston Dog Park

Address: 1101 Lowell-Spencer Mountain Road

Phone: 704-922-2160

Hours: Open 7:00 am to sunset.

GREENSBORO

Bark Park Dog Park

Address: 3905 Nathanael Green Drive

Hours: Open 8:00 am to sunset.

GREENVILLE

Greenville Dog Park

Address: 1703 River Drive

K

KERNERSVILLE

Kernersville Dog Park

Address: 702 West Mountain Street

Phone: 336-996-3062

KURE BEACH

Gurney Hood Dog Park

Address: K Avenue

M

MEBANE

Paws 4 Ever

Address: 6311 A Nicks Road

Phone: 919-304-2300 ext 233

Hours: Open 8:00 am to sunset.

Fees: $50.00 annually.

N

NEW BERN

Down East Dog Park

Address: 332 Glenburnie Drive

Phone: 252-639-2901

Fees: $35.00 annually or $15.00 monthly or $10.00 one weekend permit.

R

RALEIGH

Carolina Pines Community Dog Park

Address: 2305 Lake Wheeler Road

Millbrook Dog Park

Address: 1905 Spring Forest Road

Oakwood Dog Park

Address: 910 Brookside Drive

RURAL HALL

Horizons Happy Hounds Dog Park
Address: 2835 Memorial Industrial School Road
Hours: Open 7:00 am to sunset.

RUTHERFORDTON

Four Paws Kingdom
Address: 335 Lazy Creek Drive
Phone: 828-287-7324
Hours: 8:30 am to 1:00 pm and 2:00 pm to 6:00 pm April through November.

ST. STEPHENS

St. Stephen's Dog Park
Address: 2247 36th Avenue NE
Hours: 8:00 am to 6:00 pm (November – February), 8:00 am to 7:00 pm (March -October), 8:00 am to 8:00 pm (April – September). Closed Tuesday – Thursday.
Fees: $20.00 annually.

STEELE CREEK

Berewick District Dog Park

Address: Dixie River Road

Hours: Open 7:30 am to sunset.

T

TOWN OF CARY

Town of Cary Dog Park

Address: 2050 Northwest Maynar Road

Phone: 919-469-4064

Hours: Open 7:00 am to 10:00 pm.

Fees: $5.00 for a visitor, $40.00 annually for one dog, $60.00 a year for multiple dogs.

W

WAKE FOREST

Flaherty Dog Park

Address: 1226 North White Street

Phone: 919-554-6180

Hours: Open sunrise to sunset.

WAYNESVILLE

Waynesville Pepsi Dog Park

Address: Vance Street and Howell Mill Road

WILMINGTON

Ogden Dog Park

Address: Market Street

Phone: 910-798-7620

OHIO

A

AKRON
Akron Dog Park
Address: 499 Memorial Parkway

AMELIA
Great Amelia Paw Park
Address: Robin Way and Canary Lane

ANDERSON
Kellogg Dog Field
Address: 6701 Kellogg Avenue

ASHLAND

Peppy Paws Pooch Park

Address: 1046 County Road 1175

Phone: 419-606-2395

Hours: Daylight Hours.

Fees: $239.00 annually, $20.00 day pass, or $150.00 Monday through Friday annually, or $199.00 weekend annually.

AVON LAKE

Park 4 Paws Avon Lake Dog Park

Address: 33401 Webber Road

Hours: Open 7:00 am to 9:00 pm.

B

BLANCHESTER

Tom Harvey Memorial Dog Park

Address: 11704 Route 730

Hours: Open sunrise to sunset.

BRUNSWICK

Brunswick Dog Park

Address: Cross Creek Drive

C

CANAL FULTON

Canal Fulton Dog Park

Address: Butterbridge Road

CELINA

Celina Rotary Dog Park

Address: West Bank Road

Hours: Open sunrise to 11:00 pm.

CINCINNATI

Mt. Airy Forrest Dog Park

Address: Westwood Northern Boulevard

Otto Armleder Dog Park
Address: Wooster Pike

Red Dog Park
Address: 5081 Madison Road
Phone: 513-733-3647
Hours: Open sunrise to sunset.

CIRCLEVILLE
AW Marion State Dog Park
Address: 7317 Warner Huffer Road
Phone: 740-869-3124

CLEVELAND
Tremont Valley-Clark Field Dog Park
Address: West 11th Street and Clark Avenue

COLLEGE CORNER

Hueston Woods State Dog Park
Address: 6301 Park Office Road
Phone: 513-523-6347

COLUMBUS

Big Walnut Dog Park
Address: 5000 East Livingstone Avenue
Hours: Open 7:00 am to 11:00 pm

Three Creeks Dog Park
Address: Spangler Road

Wheeler Memorial Dog Park
Address: 725 Thurber Drive West
Hours: Open 7:00 am to 11:00 pm.

CORTLAND

Cooperation Station Dog Park

Address: 1439 State Route 305

CUYAHOGA FALLS

Keyser Dog Park

Address: 851 West Bath Road

D

DAYTON

Montgomery County Bark Park

Address: 6794 Webster Street

Hours: Open sunrise to sunset.

DEERFIELD

Schappacher Dog Park

Address: 4686 Old Irwin Simpson Road

Hours: Daylight hours.

DELAWARE

Bark Til Dark Dog Park
Address: 1277 Hills Miller Road
Phone: 740-369-9170
Hours: April through October 8:30 am to 8:30 pm (Monday-Friday) and 8:30 am to 5:00 pm (Saturday-Sunday); November through March 8:30 am to sunset (Monday-Friday) and 10:00 am to 6:00 pm (Saturday and Sunday).
Fees: $18.00 per month.

Companion Club Dog Park
Address: 6306 Home Road
Hours: 10:00 am to 8:00 pm (Monday-Friday), 10:00 am to 6:00 pm (Saturday and Sunday).
Fees: $395.00 annually or $25.00 visitor pass.

D

DUBLIN

Nando's Dog Park
Address: Cosgray Road and Shier Rings Road

E

EASTLAKE

Woodland Dog Park

Address: Lakeshore Boulevard

F

FAYETTE

Harrison Lake State Dog Park

Address: 26246 Harrison Lake Road

Phone: 419-237-2593

FINDLAY

K-9 Field Of Dreams

Address: Township Road 208

Phone: 419-425-7275

FORT THOMAS

Fort Thomas Dog Park

Address: Mayfield Avenue

Hours: Open sunrise to sunset.

G

GAHANA

Pooch Playground

Address: 6547 Clark State Road

Hours: Open sunrise to sunset.

Pooch Playground Dog Park

Address: 940 Pizzurro Park Way

Hours: Open sunrise to sunset.

GRANVILLE

Granville Village Dog Park

Address: Wildwood and Broadway

H

HAMILTON TOWNSHIP

Bigfoot Run Dog Park

Address: Morrow-Cozaddale Road

HURON TOWNSHIP

Osborn Dog Park

Address: Hull Road

Fees: $15.00 annually (residents), $20.00 annually (non-residents).

L

LAKEWOOD

Lakewood Dog Park

Address: Valley Parkway

Hours: Open 8:00 am to 9:00 pm.

LEWIS CENTER

Alum Creek Dog Park

Address: Hollenback Road

M

MARION

Kaufman Dog Park

Address: 2375 East Harding Highway

Hours: Open sunrise to sunset.

MASILLON

Furnas Dog Park

Address: 900 17th Street NE and Hankins

Phone: 330-832-1621

MEDINA

Memorial Dog Park

Address: East Homestead Drive

MENTOR

Mentor Dog Park

Address: Hopkins Road

Hours: Daylight hours.

MIAMI TOWNSHIP

Bark Park at Miami Meadows

Address: 1546 State Route 131

MT. STERLING

Address: 20635 State Park Road 20

Phone: 740-869-3124

N

NEWTON

Wags Park

Address: 3810 Church Street

Phone: 513-561-7867

Hours: Open 10:00 am to 8:00 pm.

P

PORTAGE LAKE

Portage Lake Dog Park

Address: 5031 Manchester Road

Phone: 330-644-2220

Hours: Open sunrise to sunset.

S

SOUTH EUCLID

Quarry Dog Park

Address: South Belvoir and Monticello

Hours: Open sunrise to sunset.

SPRINGBORO

Springboro Dog Park

Address: 75 West Central Avenue

Phone: 937-748-1378

Fees: $50.00 annually or $30.00 summer or $15.00 monthly.

SPRINGFIELD

Wiggley Field

Address: 1545 Pumphouse Road

Phone: 937-328-7275

ST. MARY'S

Fur Ever Friends Dog Park

Address: 834 Edgewater Drive

STOW

Bow Wow Beach Dog Park

Address: 5027 Stow Road

Hours: Open sunrise to sunset.

SYMMES TOWNSHIP

Symmes Township

Address: 11600 Lebanon Road

T

TIPP CITY
Address: Kyle Street

TWINSBURG
Liberty Dog Park
Address: Liberty Road
Phone: 330-963-8722

W

WEELSTON
Lake Alma State Dog Park
Address: Lake Alma Road
Phone: 740-384-4474

WEST CHESTER
Wiggle Field Dog Park
Address: VOA Park Drive
Hours: Open 8:00 am to dark.

WESTERVILLE

Brooksedge Bark Park

Address: 708 Park Meadow Road

WOOSTER

Schellin Dog Park

Address: Maple Street

X

XENIA

Francis Kennels Private Dog Park

Address: 1984 Lower Bellbrook Road

Phone: 937-374-1636

Xenia Scout Burnell-Garbrecht Dog Park

Address: 210 Fairground Road

Phone: 937-562-7440

PENNSYLVANIA

A

ALLISON PARK

North Dog Park

Address: Walter Road and Lake Shore Drive

Phone: 724-935-1766

B

BEAVER FALLS

Brady's Run Dog Park

Address: 526 Brady's Run Road

BETHLEHEM

Monocacy Dog Park

Address: 259 Illick's Mill Road

C

COLMAR

Dog Town Indoor Dog Park

Address: 252 Bethlehem Pike

Phone: 267-308-0459

Hours: 10:00 am to noon (big dogs) and 1:00 pm to 3:00 pm (small dogs) Saturday.

Fees: $10.00 for the two hour play time.

CRAFTON

Thornburg Dog Park

Address: Ruthers Road

Hours: Open sunrise to sunset.

CRANBERRY

Rotary Dog Park

Address: Park Road

E

EDINBORO

Howlabaloo Dog Park

Address: 11290 Lay Road

Hours: 8:00 am to 8:00 pm (April-October), 8:00 am to 6:00 pm (November-March). Closed Tuesday and Thursday until noon.

Fees: $269.00 annually or $29.00 monthly or $9.00 daily.

F

FISHTOWN

Pop's Playground Dog Park

Address: Hazard and Collin Street

FORT WASHINGTON

Mondaug Bark Park

Address: 1130 Camphill Road

FRANKLIN PARK

Misty Pines Dog Park

Address: 2523 Wexford Bayne Road

Hours: 8:00 am to 5:00 pm (Monday-Saturday and 8:00 am to 8:30 pm (Tuesday & Thursday).

Fees: $5.00 for two hours or $75.00 for a six month pass.

FREEDOM

Lucky Paws Dog Park and Pool

Address: 2273 Lovi Road

Hours: 3:00 pm to sunset (Monday-Friday) and 9:00 am to sunset (Weekends).

Fees: $10.00 for a day pass or $95.00 annually.

G

GREENSBURG

See Spot Run Dog Park

Address: 1206 South Main Street

Phone: 724-836-7768

H

HATFIELD

Hatfield Dog Park

Address: 2500 North Chestnut Street

Phone: 215-855-0900

Hours: Open sunrise to sunset.

HERMITAGE

Hillcrest Dog Park

Address: 2619 East State Street

Phone: 724-347-5100

HIGHLAND PARK

Highland Park Dog Park

Address: Highland Avenue and Reservoir Drive

HORSHAM

Horsham Dog Park

Address: 1051 Horsham Road

I

INDIANA

The Charlie Douglas Dog Park

Address: 500 Ben Franklin Road South

Phone: 724-349-3310

Hours: Open 24 hours per day.

Fees: $10.00 per week, $30.00 per month, $75.00 per quarter or $295.00 annually.

L

LANCASTER

Buchanan Park Dog Park

Address: Buchanan and College Avenue

Overlook Dog Park

Address: 2215 Fruitville Pike

Hours: Open sunrise to sunset.

Fees: $35.00 annually

LEWISBURG

Turtle Creek Dog Park

Address: Supplee Mill Road

LOWER PAXTON TOWNSHIP

Happy Tails Dog Park

Address: Dowhower and Union Deposit Roads

M

MALVERN

Canine Creature Comforts

Address: 81 Lancaster Avenue

Phone: 610-296-8407

Hours: Noon to 1:00 pm (puppies under 5 months) and 1:00 pm to 3:00 pm (older dogs).

Fees: $10.00 for one visit or $45.00 for 5 play sessions or $85.00 for 10 play sessions.

MCKEESPORT
White Oak Dog Park
Address: 3 Muse Lane
Phone: 412-678-3774

MECHANICSBURG
Greenlin Kennel Pet Resort
Address: 710 Eppley Resort
Phone: 717-766-8622
Fees: $50.00 annually

Lower Allen Community Dog Park
Address: 4075 Lisburn Road
Hours: Open sunrise to sunset.

MIDDLETOWN
Greenlin Kennel Pet Resort
Address: 600 Schoolhouse Road
Phone: 717-944-9848
Hours: Open sunrise to sunset.
Fees: $50.00 annually

MONROEVILLE

Heritage Dog Park

Address: 2364 Saunders Station Road

N

NAZARETH

Nazareth Borough Dog Park

Address: Black Rock Road

NEWTON SQUARE

Family Pet Resort Dog Park

Address: 3921 Miller Road

Phone: 610-325-7297

Hours: Open Saturdays.

NORTH WALES

Bark Park

Address: Welsh Road

P

PENN HILLS

Penn Hills Dog Park
Address: Jefferson Road

PHILADELPHIA

I-95 Dog Park
Address: Front and Chestnut

Chester Avenue Dog Park
Address: Chester Avenue and 48th Street
Hours: Open 7:00 am to 9:00 pm (Monday-Friday) and 9:00 am to 9:00 pm (weekends) and 11:00 am to 7:00 pm (holidays)
Fees: $62.50 annually

Eastern State Dog Park
Address: Corinthian Avenue and Brown Street

Mario Lanza Dog Park
Address: Catharine Street

Orianna Hill Dog Park
Address: 900 North Orianna Street
Fees: $30.00 annually

Passyunk Square Dog Park
Address: 1200 Wharton Street

Pretzel Dog Park
Address: Silverwood and Rector Street

Schuylkill River Park Dog Run
Address: 11th Street
Hours: Open 6:00 am to 10:00 pm

Triangle Dog Park
Address: Under 95 where Aramingo, East Girard and Fletcher meet.

PHOENIXVILLE

Reservoir Dogs Park
Address: Fillmore Street and Franklin Avenue

Reynolds Dog Park
Address: 100 Longford Road

PITTSBURGH

Doglogic Indoor Dog Park
Address: 1405 Saw Mill Run Boulevards
Phone: 412-882-0676
Hours: Small dogs- Saturday 10:00 am to noon & Big dogs- Sunday 10:00 am to noon.
Fees: $6.00 day use or $40.00 pack of ten.

Hartwood Acres County Dog Park
Address: Middle Road
Phone: 412-767-9200

Riverview Dog Park
Address: 159 Riverview Avenue
Phone: 412-323-7209

The Dog Stop Indoor Dog Park
Address: 1140 Washington Boulevard
Phone: 412-361-0911
Hours: 5:00 pm to 7:00 pm (Monday-Friday) and 12:00 pm to 4:00 pm (Saturday).
Fees: $5.00 day pass, $25.00 month pass or $200.00 annually.

S

SCRANTON

Connell Dog Park
Address: Near 800 Gibbons Street

SEWICKLEY HEIGHTS

Sewickley Heights Borough Park Off Leash Area

Address: Fern Hollow Road

Phone: 412-741-7536

SHIPPENSBURG

Bubba's Happy Tails Dog Park

Address: 304 Britton Road

SOUTH PARK

South Dog Park

Address: Corrigan Drive

Phone: 412-835-4810

SQUIRREL HILL

Upper Frick Dog Park

Address: Beechwood Boulevard

STATE COLLEGE

Tudek Dog Park

Address: Park Crest Lane

U

UPPER DARBY TOWNSHIP

Kent Dog Park

Address: 3900 block of Bridge Street

Hours: Open 8:00 am to sunset.

Fees: $20.00 for the first year and $10.00 annually afterward.

W

WARMINSTER

Warminster Township Bark Park

Address: 300 Veterans Way

Phone: 215-443-5428

WASHINGTON

Dogs Rule Dog Store and Playground

Address: 1445 Washington Road

Phone: 724-222-7020

WEST CHESTER

Applebrook Inn Pet Resort Dog Park

Address: 1691 West Strasburg Road

Phone: 610-692-7178

Hours: Open 7:00 am to 7:00 pm.

Fees: $5.00 day use, $20.00 monthly, $45.00 quarterly, $70.00 semi-annual, or $100.00 annually.

WEST GOSHEN

Roonie's Canine Corner

Address: Pottstown Pike

Phone: 610-696-5266

Hours: Closed Monday through Thursday from 10:00 am to 11:30 am for maintenance.

WEST PITTSTON

The Garden Village Dog Park

Address: Exeter Avenue

Hours: Open sunrise to sunset.

WEXFORD

K9 Kingdom Indoor Adventure Park

Address: 155 Lake Drive

Phone: 724-935-3647

Hours: 5:00 pm to 7:00 pm (weekdays) and 10:00 am to 3:00 pm (weekends).

Fees: $6.00

WILLOW GROVE

Willow Grove Pooch Park

Address: 1150 Easton Road

Phone: 215-659-3441

Hours: Saturdays noon to 2:00 pm (big dogs) and 10:00 am to noon (small dogs)

Fees: $5.00 day pass ($10.00 initial registration fee).

WYNCOTE

Curtis Dog Park

Address: Church Road and Greenwood Avenue

Phone: 215-887-6200- ext 227

Hours: 8:00 am to 8:30 pm (May-August), 8:00 am to 6:00 pm (September-April).

Y

YORK

Canine Meadows

Address: Dellinger Road

Hours: Open 8:00 am to dusk.

RHODE ISLAND

B
BARRINGTON
Barrington Dog Park
Address: Haines Park Road

N
NEWPORT
Newport Dog Park
Address: Connell Highway
Hours: Open 6:00 am to 9:00 pm.

P
PROVIDENCE
Dexter Dog park
Address: Dexter Street

Gano Street Dog Park
Address: Power and Gano

W

WARWICK

Warwick Dog Park

Address: Asylum

SOUTH CAROLINA

C

CHARLESTON

Ackerman Park Dog Run
Address: 55 Sycamore Drive

Hampton Park Dog Run
Address: Rutledge Avenue and Grove Street

Hazel Parker Park Dog Run
Address: 70 East Bay Street

James Island County Dog Park
Address: 871 Riverland Drive
Hours: Closed Wednesday mornings.
Fees: $1.00 per person admission.

COLUMBIA

Barking Lot Dog Park
Address: Bush River Road
Fees: $40.00 annually (residents), $55.00 annually (non-residents) plus parking fees.

Doggie Park
Address: Humane Lane

Lake Carolina Dog Park
Address: 971 Lake Carolina Boulevard

Sesqui Dog Park
Address: 9564 Two Notch Road
Hours: 8:00 am to 6:00 pm
Fees: $25.00 annually, or $4.00 day pass plus $2.00 per adult.

F

FLORENCE

Florence Dog Park

Address: SC South 21-508

G

GREENVILLE

Canine Corner Cleveland Dog Park

Address: 126 Woodland Way

Hours: Open sunrise to sunset.

GREER

Six Wags of Greer

Address: 3669 North Highway 14

Phone: 864-895-5355

H

HILTON HEAD ISLAND

Address: William Hilton Parkway

Hours: Open sunrise to sunset.

I

ISLE OF THE PALMS

Bark Park Dog Park

Address: 29th Street

Hours: Open sunrise to sunset. Closed Wednesday 10:00 am to noon.

K

KIAWAH ISLAND

Kiawah Island's Beach Off Leash Area

Address: Kiawah Island Parkway

Hours: Open sunrise to sunset.

M

MOUNT PLEASANT

Palmetto Islands County Dog Park
Address: 444 Needlerush Parkway

MYRTLE BEACH

Barc Park
Address: Mallard Lake Drive
Phone: 843-918-2390
Hours: Open sunrise to sunset.

North End Dog Park
Address: Bypass from 62nd Avenue North
Phone: 843-918-2390
Hours: Open sunrise to sunset.

N

NORTH CHARLESTON

Wannamaker County Dog Park
Address: 8888 University Boulevard
Phone: 843-572-7275

TENNESSEE

B

BARTLETT

Bartlett Dog Park
Address: 5220 Shelter Run Lane

C

CHATTANOOGA

Chattanooga Chew Chew Canine Park
Address: 1801 Carter Street

CLARKSVILLE

Clarksville Bark Park
Address: 1190 Cumberland Drive
Phone: 931-645-7476

F

FRANKLIN

Maggies Bark Park

Address: 138 Claude Yates Drive

Hours: Open sunrise to sunset.

G

GERMANTOWN

Forgery Dog Park

Address: 1695 Riverdale Road

Hours: Open sunrise to sunset.

Fees: $40.00 annually (resident) and $60.00 annually (non-resident).

GOODLETTSVILLE

Fenway's Dog Park

Address: 745 Caldwell Lane

J

JOHNSON CITY

Willow Springs Dog Park
Address: 1200 Huffine Road
Fees: $35.00 annually.

K

KINGSPORT

Dogwood Park
Address: 800 Granby Road
Fees: $10.00 annually (residents) and $15.00 annually (non-residents).

KNOXVILLE

Dogwood Dog Park
Address: 4901 Bradshaw Road

Pet Safe Dog Park
Address: 2065 Rifle Range Drive

Pet Safe Village Dog Park
Address: 10424 Electric Avenue
Phone: 865-777-3647
Hours: 5:00 pm to sunset (Monday-Friday) and 3:00 pm to sunset (weekends).

M
MURFREESBORO BARK PARK
Murfreesboro Bark Park
Address: West College Street
Hours: Open sunrise to sunset.

N
NASHVILLE
Centennial Dog Park
Address: 31st and Parthenon

Shelby Dog Park
Address: South 20th and Shelby
Hours: Open sunrise to 8:00 pm.

Warner Dog Park
Address: Vaughn Road
Hours: Open sunrise to sunset.

VERMONT

B

BURLINGTON

Starr Farm Dog Park

Address: Starr Farm Road

Hours: 8:00 am to 8:00 pm (April- October) and 8:00 am to 6:00 pm (November-March)

Urban Reserve Off Leash Dog Park

Address: Lake Street

H

HARTFORD

Watson Upper Valley Dog Park

Address: Route 14 West

Hours: Open sunrise to sunset (April-October).

M

MANCHESTER

Manchester Dog Park
Address: Rec Park Road

VIRGINIA

A

ALEXANDRIA

Beatley Library Dog Park
Address: 5000 Block of Duke Street

Ben Brennan Dog Park
Address: Brennan Park Drive

Dog Run Park at Carlyle
Address: 450 Andrew's Lane
Phone: 703-746-5484

Grist Mill Dog Park
Address: 4710 Mt. Vernon Memorial Highway
Hours: Open sunrise to sunset.

Montgomery Dog Park
Address: Fairfax and 1st Street

Simpson Stadium Dog Park
Address: Monroe Avenue and Leslie

ANNANDALE
Mason District Dog Park
Address: Alpine Drive
Hours: Open sunrise to sunset.

ARLINGTON
Fort Barnard Dog Park
Address: 2101 South Pollard Street
Hours: Open sunrise to sunset.

Fort Ethan Allen Dog Park
Address: 3829 North Stafford Street
Hours: Open sunrise to sunset.

Towers Dog Park
Address: 801 South Scott Street
Hours: Open sunrise to 11:00 pm.

Utah Dog Park
Address: 3191 South Utah Street
Hours: Open sunrise to sunset.

ASHLAND

Hanover Dog Park
Address: 13017 Taylor Complex Lane
Hours: Open 9:00 am to 4:30 pm (Monday, Tuesday, Thursday, Friday) and 9:00 am to 6:00 pm (Wednesday) and 10:00 am to 3:30 pm (Saturday). Closed Sunday.

CHANTILLY

Quinn Farm Dog Park
Address: 15150 Old Lee Road
Hours: Open sunrise to sunset.

CHARLOTTESVILLE

Azalea Dog Park

Address: Old Lynchburg Road

Hours: Open 6:00 am to 9:00 pm.

CHESAPEAKE

Chesapeake City Dog Park

Address: 500 Greenbriar Parkway

Western Branch Dog Park

Address: Portsmouth Boulevard

CLARENDON

Clarendon Dog Park

Address: 1299 Herndon and 13th Street

Hours: Open sunrise to sunset.

F

FREDERICKSBURG

Fredericksburg Dog Park

Address: Kenmore Avenue

Hours: Open sunrise to sunset.

H

HAMPTON

Ridgway Bark Park

Address: 85 East Mercury Boulevard

Hours: Open sunrise to sunset.

Fees: $10.00 annually.

Sandy Bottom Bark Park

Address: Center Parkway and Big Bethel Road

Hours: Open sunrise to sunset.

Fees: $10.00 annually.

HERNDON

Chandon Dog Park

Address: 900 Palmer Drive

Hours: Open sunrise to sunset.

L

LEESBURG

Leesburg Dog Park

Address: Davis Court

Hours: Open sunrise to sunset.

The Leesburg Canine Country Club

Address: 22025 Evergreen Mills Road

Phone: 703-722-2275

Hours: Open sunrise to 9:00 pm and Open House on most Sundays from 1:00 pm to 3:00 pm. Closed Christmas and Thanksgiving.

Fees: $55.00 application fee plus $270 annually or $120.00 for 10 day passes or $180.00 for the small dog area.

M

MARTINSVILLE

Henry County SPCA Dog Park
Address: 132 Joseph Martin Highway
Phone: 276-638-7297
Hours: Open daylight hours.
Fees: $15.00 annually to use the park and be a member of the SPCA.

N

NORFOLK

Ballantine and Tait Terrace Dog Park
Address: Ballantine Boulevard and Tait Terrace

Colonial Greenway Dog Park
Address: Llewellyn Avenue and Delaware Street

Lafayette Dog Park
Address: Lafayette Boulevard

Stockley Gardens Dog Park
Address: Stockley and Maury Avenue

O

OAKTON

Blake Lane Dog Park
Address: 10033 Blake Lane
Hours: Open sunrise to sunset.

R

RESTON

Address: 11300 Baron Cameron Avenue
Hours: Open sunrise to sunset.

RICHMOND

Barker Field Dog Park
Address: Pump House Drive

Church Hill Dog Park
Address: East Grace Street

Phideaux Field
Address: 4401 Forest Hill Avenue
Phone: 804-233-4371

Ruff House Dog Park
Address: 3401 Courthouse Road
Hours: Open 7:30 am to sunset.

S

SALEM

Six Wags Dog Park
Address: 1832 Apperson Drive
Phone: 540-375-9247
Hours: Open 6:30 am to 7:00 pm (Monday-Friday) and 8:30 am to 3:00 pm (Saturday). Closed Sunday.
Fees: $250.00 annually, $30.00 monthly or $5.00 day use.

SPRINGFIELD

South Run Dog Park
Address: 7550 Reservation Drive
Hours: Open sunrise to sunset.

V

VIENNA

A Dog's Day Out
Address: 2800 Gallows Road
Phone: 703-698-3647
Hours: Open 7:00 am to 7:00 pm (Monday-Friday) and 9:00 am to 6:00 pm (Saturday and Sunday).

Vienna Dog Park
Address: 700 Courthouse Road
Hours: Open sunrise to sunset.

W

WILLIAMSBURG

Waller Mill Dog Park

Address: Airport Road

Phone: 757-259-3760

Fees: $15.00 (resident) or $50.00 (non-resident) or $2.00 day pass.

WINCHESTER

Winchester Dog Park

Address: Maple Street

Fees: $18.00 (resident) and $24.00 (non-resident)

WASHINGTON DC

Newark Street Dog Park
Address: 39th and Newark Streets
Phone: 202-673-7647

S and T Street Dog Park
Address: 17th and S Streets NW
Phone: 202-673-7647

Kingsman Field Dog Park
Address: 13th and D Streets
Phone: 202-673-7647

Historic Congressional Cemetery Dog Walk
Address: 1801 East Street
Hours: Closed 10:00 am to 3:00 pm Saturday and Sunday.
Fees: Donate to the Cemetery Association $200 per year and $50.00 registration.

WEST VIRGINIA

C

CHARLESTON

Ruth Raferty Peyton Dog Park

Address: Washington and Maxwell Street

Hours: Open sunrise to sunset.

E

ELEANOR

Eleanor Dog Park

Address: Putnam County Fairgrounds

H

HURRICANE

Valley Dog Park

Address: 2 Valley Road

M

MORGANTOWN

Stanley's Spot Dog Park

Address: Decker's Creek Trail

Phone: 304-296-8356

Hours: Open sunrise to sunset.

Every effort was made to bring you accurate information. This book focuses on only fenced and recognized dog parks in the United States. If I missed a recognized dog park in your area, I would love to hear from you. I may be reached via email dtaber@embarqmail.com